THE INDIAN OCEAN POLITICS

THE INDIAN OCEAN POLITICS

Dr. Ajit Raizada

1994
Sharada Publishing House
Delhi - 110052

First Published 1994

ISBN : 81-85616-19-1

Published by
B.L. Bansal
for SHARADA PUBLISHING HOUSE
(Publishers on India's Past and Present)
E-239, Shastri Nagar, Delhi-110052
Phone : 7516539

Laser Typesetting by
Akriti Computers
B-5/98, Paschim Vihar, New Delhi - 110063
Phone : 5587403, 5584110

Printed at:
Raj offset Printers
Ajadpur, Delhi

Contents

Preface

The present work is the revised and updated version of my post-doctoral thesis submitted for the award of D.Litt. degree to Vikram University, Ujjain.

In recent years the Indian Ocean region has been accorded enormous importance. Important developments in the region have been a constant concern for the affected states which include the Super Powers and India. One reason why scholars - particularly those specialising in international relations, strategic studies, and foreign policy - have increasingly begun to think in terms of an Indian Ocean region is because the policy makers themselves are approaching issues in that area in a more comprehensive fashion.

The present work is an attempt to examine the various issues and problems raised and discussed within the framework of the Indian Ocean region. It begins with a preliminary quest for a feasible methodology of dealing with theoretical aspects formulated for the concept of an Indian Ocean region. It reviews and assesses the available literature in the relevant field of study.

The chapter on Super Power interests in the region explores the major political and other factors at work and tries to bring out the different phases and strategies adopted by the Super Powers to maintain their stronghold in the area.

The study also takes into account the political objectives of India in the Indian Ocean region and analyses India's options regarding its security problems. It then moves on to examine the proposals for a peace zone as enunciated and developed by the regional states.

An effort has been made to size up the potential of the policies so far pursued by the United Nations, the non-aligned nations and the Super Powers and also to make an assessment of their effectiveness.

I am grateful to Professor R.C. Dube, former Head of the Political Science and Public Administration Department, Dr. Harisingh Gour University, Sagar, who gave some very valuable suggestions. I must also record my thanks to Professor R.S. Gautam, former Head of the Political Science Department, Vikram University, Ujjain whose understanding of the subject made my own perceptions clearer.

Needless to add that the work owes its completion mainly to the inspiring company of my wife, Dr. Seema Raizada who teaches English Literature but has an avid interest in the happenings on planet Earth.

Bhopal AJIT RAIZADA
17th September, 1993

CHAPTER I

Theoretical Orientation

There is considerable imprecision concerning the term theory; to many it means a hypothesis, or even an agrument that can be in some way verified (or falsified) by the empirical material. But this argument is fundamentally flawed. The devices that we use to explain empirical material can, following Waltz,[1] be divided into hypotheses and theories; each of these has a very different relationship to the empirical material. According to a very common view of this relationship, a theory is merely a collection of verified hypotheses, or laws, that apply to a particular behavioural phenomenon. This view is specially powerful when it has what can be called a technology utility, that is, verified hypotheses which offer us ways of achieving certain goals. The most obvious example of this is the knowledge derived from correlation coefficients. As Waltz writes, "It is then easy to believe that a real causal connection has been identified and measured, to think that the relationship between an independent and a dependent variable has been established, and to forget that something has been said only about dots on a piece of paper and the regression line drawn through them."[2] While high correlation coefficients may be very useful in practical terms, they do not constitute an explanation. This is, then, a confusion of descriptive and explanatory knowledge.

But theories are not collections of verified hypotheses or laws, but they are devices that explain an empirical relationship. This position should not be confused with the positivist position so powerfully attacked by Keat and Urry,[3] since theories may consist of non-empirical observations. Under this view, theories differ fundamentally from hypotheses and laws in terms of their link with the empirical material. Whereas we can assess hypotheses and laws in terms of their validity and thereby construct a direct link between them and empirical data, we evaluate theories in terms of the amount of behaviour that they can explain. Of course, theories may lead to the deduction of hypotheses, which may then be subjected to examination against the empirical data, but theories themselves cannot be proved to be true or false. They are either more or less powerful in their explanation, with the concept of explanatory power measured in terms of a theory's ability to explain more observed behaviour than its rivals. The criterion of empirical verification, therefore, applies to hypotheses and laws and not to theories. Hence one theory is replaced not by a 'truer' one, or by one that contains more hypotheses, but by one with more explanatory power, one that can better explain the relationship between theory and empirical material in this indirect way. Therefore, while theories are neither true nor false, they do have the requirement of relating to verified hypotheses. In this way they can be distinguished from normative theories, that is, theories that deal with questions of what should be the case. Since facts do not speak for themselves, mere verified hypotheses cannot constitute explanations. Herein, of course, lies one of the major problems in the methodology of history since the existence of 'facts' can in no way lead the historians to induce an explanation. This is not to say that historians do not derive explanations, but they clearly must do so on the basis of deducing from theories and to link these to causal processes.

A paradigm provides exactly the kind of criteria that allows the scholars in a field to distinguish between relevant and irrelevant facts. In this sense it has a direct relationship to the empirical material, in that it defines the relevant facts and thereby the central issues to be explained by theory. As Kuhn writes : "Paradigms gain their status because they are more successful than their competitors in solving a few problems that the group of practitioners has come to recognise as acute."[4] This is the way in which theory, in a normal science, relates most directly to the empirical material. Indeed, paradigms are not replaced by more accurate ones, they are superseded by paradigms that explain more of the observable behaviour. Since paradigms themselves determine the relevance of empirical material, competing paradigms may exist with each paradigm focussing on different behaviour and different questions. Kuhn argues that normal science is not characterised by disputes between competing paradigms, rather it sees one paradigm dominating the subject-area. It must be stressed that Kuhn is not a relativist, although this is something that he has often been accused of. Kuhn does not argue that it is impossible to choose between competing theories, precisely because there exists a link between theory, hypotheses and empirical material. Thus, although competing paradigms do not focus on exactly the same material and do not see exactly the same questions as central to the task of explanation, there is a corpus of behaviour that no explanation can ignore. In principle, the resolution of disputes between competing paradigms is possible, thus avoiding the problem of relativism.

Since the emergence of International Relations as a discipline in the period immediately following the First World War, it is normally argued that two major phases have existed. In chronological order, these phases were: idealism, which dominated the discipline in the inter-war years, and realism, which received its initial statement in E.H.Carr's *The Twenty Years' Crisis*[5] and which characterised the discipline from the period of the Second World War to the 1960s. Since the 1960s, realism has come under attack from an approach called behaviouralism. The current situation is one in which the realist paradigm, or versions of it, has strong adherents in the discipline, being opposed by what can be called the transnationalist paradigm. In the 1990s it is simply not the case that either one of these approaches dominates the discipline, as will be disucssed below.

Idealism was, naturally, largely preoccupied with avoiding a repetiton of wars such as the First World War. As Bull has argued, the distinctive characteristic of idealism was the belief in progress: "the belief, in particular, that the system of international relations that had given rise to the First World War was capable of being transformed into a fundamentally more peaceful and just world order; that under the impact of the awakening of democracy, the growth of 'the international mind', the development of the League of Nations, the good works of men of peace or the enlightenment spread by their own teachings, it was in fact being transformed; and that their responsibility was to assist this march of progress to overcome the ignorance, the prejudices, the ill-will, and the sinister interests that stood in its way."[6] Given this orientation, the discipline concentrated on developing and publicising techniques for the peaceful resolution of crisis. Hence, considerable attention was paid to international law and to international organisations. Rational decision-makers wished to avoid war. So, the task of International Relations was to provide the mechanisms necessary to ensure this. The First World War was seen as occurring because of misperception and accident. The League of Nations was, therefore, based on assumption as to the role of mediation and the peace-enchancing characteristics of democracy. Combined with these beliefs was the powerful manifesto of Wilson's Fourteen Points. Taken together these viewpoints formed the basis of idealism.

The growing disparity between these views and real-world events in the 1930s, primarily the advent of the Second World War, led to a re-examination of this discipline. This is most cogently expresseed in Carr's *The Twenty Years' Crisis* and Morgenthau's *Politics Among Nations.*[7] Carr's book contains a most powerful attack on idealism, an attack based on the idea that the science of International Relations was in its early stages. In this period, Carr argues, any discipline is likely to be characterised by utopianism, that is by a concentration on what ought to be rather than on what is.

This critical analysis was labelled as 'realism' by Carr and its most powerful statement occurs in Morgenthau's seminal book, *Politics Among Nations*. For Morgenthau, International Relations had to start from a realisation that the international political behaviour of states had its origins in immutable laws of nature. On this basis, he offers a theory of international politics, the purpose of which is "to bring order and meaning to a mass of phenomena which without it would remain disconnected and unintelligible".[8] This theory not only has to be consistent within itself, it also has to be consistent with the facts. Here again we see the relationship between theory and empirical material; the material gives rise to the revision of theory, the theory determines the facts to be explained, yet the theory must be consistent with the major empirical developments.

Morgenthau's theory is based on six principles. The first of these is that political behaviour is governed "by objective laws that have their roots in human nature."[9] These laws cannot be altered by human beings and can therefore be challenged only at the risk of failure. Secondly, realism offers an explanation of International Relations by concentrating on power. As Morgenthau writes : "We assume that statesmen think and act in terms of interest defined as power."[10] Thirdly,realism does not endow the concept of power with one fixed meaning; power can relate to any process by which individuals seek to dominate other individuals. Fourthly,while the realist is aware of the role of morality in international political behaviour, universal moral principles cannot be applied to international relations. There can be no political morality without prudence, especially when seemingly moral action could lead to the destruction of the state. Fifthly, realism does not identify the moral aspirations of any one state with universal morality; hence, it can offer a means of judging all states' behaviour. Finally, the realist sees the political sphere as autonomous in that other modes of thought cannot explain the central areas of behaviour.

However, by the late 1950s realism itself was under attack from what can be called behaviouralism, a school of thought based on developing knowledge about observable behaviour. For this school of thought, realism had a fundamental epistemological flaw since it started from unobservable fixed laws of human standpoint. Although behaviouralism took many different forms, the clearest examples of it are provided by the decision-making approach started by Richard Snyder[11] and the systems-theory approach introduced by Morton Kaplan.[12] For Snyder, foreign policy behaviour was not to be explained by any rational assessments of interest defined as power (as were required by Morgenthau), but by the subjective choices, based on the definition of the situation, of the decision-makers. For Snyder, explanation did not consist of seeing these choices as examples of fixed laws of nature, but by undertaking empirical investigation to see how decision-makers defined situations.

Similarily, for Kaplan, understanding the behaviour of great powers was not be arrived at through seeing it as the characteristic behaviour of states located in an immutable web of objectives laws, but as determined by more specific, and thereby changing, characteristics of the structure of the system. Hence Kaplan constructs a series of theoretical models of the system and in later work outlined alternative theoretical models. The contrast between his work and that of Morgenthau is subtle but significant.

Behaviouralism's attack on realism was by no means universally accepted, and the realists, or, as they became known, the traditionalists, mounted a very strong counter-attack. This led to a famous debate between Bull and Kaplan.[13] A much more serious argument was the post-behaviouralist attack which had two main aspects: first, a criticism of behaviouralism's absence of moral and normative content. By concentrating on what is, and by confining theory to an explanation of this, behaviouralism is seen as being devoid of moral content. Given the role of academics in the United States in the explanation of the Vietnam War, this is an understandable criticism of behaviouralism. The second aspect of the post-behavioural critique is a rejection of the inductive approach to developing knowledge. This position is most clearly expressed in Oran Young's celebrated attack on inductivism.[14] It has also been a central argument in the critique of what is probably the best example of inductive research - Singer's Correlates of War Project.[15] In other words, this criticism argues that merely accumulating empirical evidence cannot provide the basis of explanation.

In the literature on International Relations it is common to see these differing schools of thought (idealism, realism, behaviouralism and post-behaviouralism) as competing paradigms. This, however, is an over simplification, since only the first two achieved anything like the degree of theoretical dominance in the discipline required by Kuhn's notion of a paradigm. Indeed, behaviouralism and post-behaviouralism by themselves do not necessarily focus on different aspects of International Relations than do idealism and realism. There is nothing intrinsic to behaviouralism that forces it to study anything different to that studied by realists - one can easily envisage realist behaviouralists. Thus, Kaplan and Snyder have more in common with Morgenthau or Carr than is commonly accepted. The current identity crisis, then, is not simply one based on the issue of which methodology is appropriate; it relates to the fundamental issues of what is to be studied. This can be most clearly indicated by looking at the question of the state in International Relations.

To summarise the argument thus far: International Relations, from its inception as a separate discipline to the early 1970s, was based on a state-centric power-politics framework. Thus, whilst idealists might disagree over how to get peace, each saw states as actors, and war as the central problem. While behaviouralism might criticise the methodology of realism, it still saw the central behaviour to be explained as the power-political behaviour of states. Again, post-behaviouralism might criticise either the inductiveness of much behaviouralism or the lack of any normative content, but it too was concerned with the security policies of states.

The events of the 1970s can usefully be separated into three categories: those concerned with the structure of the global system; those concerned with the units of international society; and those concerned with the processes of International Relations. Rather than discuss each in detail, a brief summary of the major events in each category is offered.

At the global level, the major event was the seeming break-up of bipolarity (US-Soviet dominance). On the one hand, this was due to the fragmentation of the two-bloc system; on the other, it resulted from the rise of other actors. Thus, many academics saw the beginnings of a trend that could lead to a multipolar (or a tripolar) world, with China, a united Western Europe, and Japan all challenging the domination of the United States and the Soviet Union. This process was seen to be all the more powerful because of the likely spread of nuclear weapons to other states. Added to this was the clear increase in the economic capabilities of great, as distinct from super powers. Finally, the superpowers themselves seemed to be engaged in a transformation of their relationship into one of detente, as marked by the Non-Proliferation Treaty, by the Berlin agreement, by the Conference on Security and Co-operation in Europe, and, above all, by the Strategic Arms Limitation Talks. In this environment the suitability of the assumptions of realism and of much power-based behaviouralism were called into question. Probably the best examples of this are Alastair Buchan's

The End of the Postwar Era,[16] and Sayom Brown's *New Forces in World Politics,*[17] both published in 1974. Each of these books talks about the end of Cold War alignments in the system, with Buchan concentrating on the new world balance of power, and Brown focussing on the disintegration of the Cold War coalitions.

At the level of the changing processes of International Relations there was one fundamental transformation which was taking place. This was the replacement of security interests by economic interests as the dominant issue in International Relations. Obviously this was related to both the rise of other economic powers and to the decline of US-Soviet rivalry. For many writers, the early 1970s saw the transformation of the East-West cleavage into a North-South cleavage. The traditional 'high politics' issues were no longer the dominant ones, rather the system was split on economic or 'low politics' issues. The clearest example was, of course, the oil crisis of 1973-74, which was seen as ushering in a new phase of International Relations.

Both of these areas of change affected the units of international society. What had been seen as essentially a state-based system was being transformed by two processes: on the one hand, the distinction between domestic and international politics was fast breaking down; on the other, new actors, non-state actors, seemed increasingly to be dominating certain, primarily economic, issue-areas. The first of these processes resulted in states no longer being able to control key areas of domestic policy. The traditional areas of economic policy were affected, and in many cases determined, by external factors. In this sense the legal concept of sovereignty was no longer as relevant as autonomy. Secondly, many of the external actors that could affect domestic issues were not states. The most obvious example was oil where OPEC and the seven large multinationals exerted a significant influence on the domestic policies of industrialised and developing states.

The effect of these changes was to call seriously into question the central assumptions of the discipline of International Relations. If states were no longer the dominant actors in certain issue-areas, if power, specifically military power, was not the focus of study, and if the units of international society were no longer autonomous in areas of central importance, then, could the state-centric view of International Relations explain the major events in the real world? The response to this situation was the development of an alternative paradigm, one usually labelled transnationalism.

This new paradigm has essentially two major components each of which takes account of part of the changes in International Relations, but which together constitute a powerful alternative to the state-centric view. The first of these relates to the growing interdependence between national societies and is best expressed in Morse's book, Modernization and the Transformation of International Relations. Morse argues that systemic economic interdependence has resulted in a situation where "traditional assumptions concerning alliances, the use of force, the role of economic diplomacy, the processes of foreign policy decision making....are....part of a paradigm of international affairs that is no longer adequate for explaining contemporary conditions."[18] For him, interdependence represents a transformation of international relations whereby foreign policies "....have become increasingly centred on low policies associated with the achievement of economic growth, but frequently intermeshed with a new form of transcendentalism that reflects the incapacity of governments to perform effectively."[19] The end result is that international politics is no longer distinct in terms of its contents; it increasingly merges with domestic politics.

The second, and major, strand of the transnational approach is that which focusses on the types of actors involved in International Relations. The main argument here is that states are no longer the dominant actors in certain issues-areas. The first detailed statement of this position was Keohane and Nye's *Transnational Relations and World Politics*,[20] in which they examined the role of a variety of non-state actors and concluded that the state-centric paradigm simply could not deal with contemporary international relations. Following this study, transnational relations developed into a minor industry, with the two most significant contributions being Mansbach, Ferguson and Lampert's *The Web of World Politics*,[21] and Mansbach and Vasquez's *In Search of Theory*.[22] The former undertook quantitative analysis to determine the percentage of non-state activity in international relations, and found that non-state actors appeared in 56 per cent of international behaviour.[23] The latter was concerned with developing an alternative to the state-centric paradigm.

However, events since 1979 appear to be particularly problematic. This is for the very simple reason that neither the state-centric nor the transnationalist paradigm seems capable of explaining the central events of international relations. Whereas the East-West split, based on the security interests of states, clearly dominated post-war international relations for twenty-five years, and whereas it was commonly accepted that this had been replaced by a North-South cleavage, based on economic issues in the mid-1970s, neither view can account for the current position. It is in this sense that the question of the return of the Cold War is perplexing. It is difficult to accept either the argument that this is merely a temporary return to the dominance of security issues, or the view that the period of the 1970s was itself an aberration. Rather, it seems that the international political system has been so transformed that economic factors are of central importance. Yet, at the same time, security issues have simply not been removed from the centre stage. Just as interdependence is so obviously a 'fact' of contemporary international relations and non-state actors are of critical importance in a wide range of international activity, so is the cleavage caused by US-Soviet rivalry a central structural feature of the international system.

Thus the new paradigm competed with the old and, for many, was clearly preferable in that it could accommodate the dominant forms of behaviour. Yet the return of features that bear more resemblance to the world of the 1950s than to the world of the 1970s calls this into question. At the same time, the state-centric approach has demonstrably failed to be able to explain the world of the 1970s. The subject of International Relations is, therefore, one in which much debate is going on as to what should be the main areas of study. While this may seem on the surface to be a sign of weakness or self-doubt, it is, in fact, a very healthy intellectual sign, becuase it makes the subject very concerned with question of relevance.

International Relations, then, has had a very interesting past. The subject has always been very explicitly concerned with explaining (rather than merely describing) the major features of international society. As these features have changed so has International Relations had to develop new theories to explain them. Since the 1960s, realism has been under attack, with the major challenge coming in the 1970s with the rise of economic factors to a position of dominance in international relations, yet, the rise of the Second Cold War in the early 1980s has led to a resurgence of realism. The study of International Relations in the second half of the 1980s looks like being exceptionally stimulating as the subject grapples with the task of explaining a dynamic, turbulent and dangerous world.

Using a division of the world into four worlds, the north-western 'First World' (countries of corporate capitalism), the north-eastern 'Second World' (countries of state socialism), the south-western 'Third World' (countries of the New International Economic Order) and the south-eastern 'Fourth World' (the countries of East and South-east Asia and Oceania), it is clear that the overwhelming majority of the member states are in the Third World. More particularly, one may perhaps say that there are around 20 countries in the First World not counting Japan, Australia and New Zealand that according to this classification would be in the Fourth World), about 15 countries in the Second World, the countries of 'really existing socialism'; about 100 countries in the Third World and about 15 again in the Fourth World - but classifications are by no means absolute and unambiguous.

The Indonesian leader Soekarno made a distinction between the OEF and NEF countries; the Old Established Forces and the New Emerging Forces. Obviously he counted Indonesia and the nonaligned movement he spearheaded so brilliantly among the latter, and the colonial powers among the former. But his world model suffered from one major weakness: there were only two actors. However, we can make use of his vocabulary and his distinction between 'old' and 'new' and 'established' and 'emerging' for what might be a more adequate description of the world, in terms of the four worlds alluded to above:

The UN dramatis personae

	Established	*Emerging*
Old	First World	Second World
New	Fourth World	Third World

First, there is the Old Established World, the First World, certainly no longer so sure of itself after decolonization and deeply shaken and interlocked in a potentially devastating nuclear conflict with the Second World, a seemingly endless series of conflict of liberation from colonialism with countries in the Third World, and the economic challenges from the countries of the Fourth World. But it still looks old and established relative to the other three worlds.

Then, there is the Second World, the Old Emerging Force. It has been on the scene for a long time now, as a challenger, from 1917 to be precise, with the founding of the Soviet Union. The second challenge is, of course, the Third World - described as a New Emerging Force. Emerging it certainly is, to the point of very high visibility (and audibility), and it is also new. There is the third challenge: the Fourth world, highly successful and nothing less than the New Established Force. There is not only the economic triumph of Japan, but also the ideological military and political strength of China.

Theoretical Bases for the Concept of an Indian Ocean Region

The academic study of the international relations of regions is largely a post-World War II development. It may be traced in part to the emergence in the 1940s and 1950s of the 'area studies' approach, inspired more by a particular interest in the affairs of a given locality than by a general interest in global affairs.[24] Furthermore, the "loosening of the bipolar world, moves toward autonomous policies by the middle range powers, and explicit efforts at fostering patterns of international collaboration in various areas of the world" all served to direct scholarly attention toward "regional foci of interaction."[25] Regions have also come to be seen as useful intermediate units of analysis at a level between individual nation-states and the world as a whole.

Generally recognized as the first to attempt such an approach was Leonard Binder in his article on the Middle East.[26] Subsequently, Michael Brecher wrote about Southern Asia;[27] William Zartman about Africa,[28] Larry Bowman about Southern Africa[29] and Donald Hellman about East Asia.[30] Louis Cantori and Steven Spiegel have explored the subject generally, taking a comparative approach to the international politics of regions.[31]

There is in the Indian Ocean a discernible 'linkage of instabilities' and it is now recognized as a distinctive 'theatre of operation'. The superpowers, in particular, have increasingly approached the Indian Ocean area as a "strategic arena" for the multiplicity of reasons. On their part, the Indian Ocean states have become increasingly sensitive to external intrusions, both as threats and as opportunities. The Indian Ocean zone-of-peace and nuclear-free-zone initiatives and the existence of the United Nations Ad Hoc Committee are evidences of an indigenous perception that the Indian Ocean is indeed a distinctive area in international politics.

Characteristic of the systems perspective are the following assumptions:

(1) A system (or regional subsystem) is more than simply the sum of its parts. It is both a 'structure' consisting of its components and the transactions among and between those parts. Much of the essence of international politics consists of linkages, interactions, reactions, and interdependence-more than the simple sum of all relevant national foreign policies.

(2) Various actors (individual decision makers, nation-states, multinational corporations, international organizations, etc.) are not only conditioned but constrained by the characteristics of the system in which they operate. In other words, "systems-level forces seems to be at work".[32] The interrelationship is dynamic and reciprocal.

(3) The examination of patterns of international relations on various levels (e.g., subnational, national,

regional) contributes to an understanding of politics at the global level.

(4) Even in the field of international relations, there are areas of coherence and orderliness in the midst of apparent conflict and diversity.

More controversial has been the issue of stability within a system, particularly as it relates to the structure and distribution of power. For example, an interesting question with respect to the Indian Ocean Subsystem is whether stability increases by the concentration and hierarchical distribution of power. The Persian Gulf core was a more stable place when the Shah's Iran dominated the power hierarchy. In South Asia, the clear predominance of India may have contributed to a more stable core area. The Southern Africa core is another case in point with a dominant South Africa. The work of David Singer and various associates provides potentially useful operational techniques for research into the question of power distribution versus stability in the Indian Ocean region.

Real World Bases for the Concept of an Indian Ocean Region

Besides the superpowers, France, Britain, Japan, and China have substantial interests in the Indian Ocean area. The diversity and relative importance of these interests is reflected in the varying degrees of coherence that is apparent in the policies of these nations towards the region. Of the four, the French policy perhaps exhibits the greatest cogency. The French remain quite active in the Indian Ocean, maintaining the largest naval presence after that of the United States and the Soviet Union. Reunion, near Mauritius, and the Island of Mayotte (Mahore) in the Comoros are administratively parts of France. It continues to station army and air force units in Djibouti. Britain's former status as the principal colonial power has left it with a host of political, economic, and strategic concerns in the region that remain of considerable importance despite its withdrawal from east of Suez. It lacks the resources to protect independently all of its interests in the Indian Ocean and, therefore, has to rely heavily on the United States for this purpose.

Although the Indian Ocean area is one of considerable economic diversity, various aspects of its economic life lend a measure of support to the notion of emerging regionality. Some of these characteristics are : similar economic profiles of most of the states of the area, movement toward subregional economic cooperation, and expansion of intraregional trade.

It was the individual country's search for national independence, together with the awareness that this was a pan-Asian (later Afro-Asian) struggle, that led to the emergence of the concept of the 'Third World'. This was eloquently given voice by Jawaharlal Nehru at the First Asian Relations Conference held in New Delhi in 1947 when he declared the "far too long have we in Asia been petitioners in Western courts and chancellories. That story must now belong to the past. We propose to stand on our legs. We do not intend to be the plaything of others".[33]

The relevance of the NAM and its ideology to the Indian Ocean region is self-evident on two counts. First, the overwhelming majority of the states of the Indian Ocean littoral and its hinterland are developing countries which belong to and identify with the Third World. Non-alignment is an ideology that aims to maximize the capacity of Third World states to act autonomously in economic and political terms. It has become the ideology that dominates the Third World's pattern of interaction with the developed countries. Its relevance to and its impact upon the actions of the states of the Indian Ocean region vis-a-vis the dominant powers cannot be overemphasized. Second, nearly forty members of the NAM belong to the Indian Ocean region (including the Persian Gulf and Red Sea littorals and landlocked countries in the hinterland, e.g., Afghanistan, Bhutan, Malawi, Nepal, Zambia, Zimbabwe). No matter how one defines the Indian Ocean region, an impressive proportion of the countries of the NAM is included.

The Economic and Strategic Interdependence of the Indian Ocean Region

The buildup of Soviet and American military forces in the Indian Ocean, following the gradual withdrawal of British forces east of Suez in the early 1970s, has generated the desire of promoting regional economic cooperation among the littoral and hinterland states of the Indian Ocean.

The failure to establish the Indian Ocean as a zone of peace is primarily due to the lack of consensus among the African and Asian states on how to eliminate the great power military presence. It is also because of conflicting interpretations of what the term means and how it to be achieved. Interpretations have included the establishment of a nuclear-free zone, the maintenance of a balance of military forces in the region that would include some external forces, and the promotion of regional economic cooperation and development.

The concepts of 'middle power' and 'strategic buffer' are usually neglected in post-1945 International Relations studies. Before applying these concepts to the Indian Ocean world, it will be helpful to define them. Martin Wight, one of the few scholars to take the concept of middle power seriously, is worth quoting at some length. According to Wight :

> Two kinds of minor power achieve an eminence which distinguishes them from the common run : regional great powers, and middle powers. Political pressures do not operate uniformly throughout the states-system, and in certain regions which are culturally united but politically divided, a subordinate international society comes into being ... In such subsystems ... there will be some states with general interests relative to the limited region and a capacity to act alone, which gives them the appearance of local great powers. Egypt, Iraq and perhaps Saudi Arabia have been great powers in the Arab world ... Similarly, South Africa may be regarded as a great power relative to Black Africa. Such regional great powers will probably be candidates, in the states-system at large, for the rank of middle power.
>
> With more precision, it might be argued that a middle power is a power with such military strength, resources and strategic position that in peace time the great powers bid for its support, and in wartime, while it has no hope of winning a war against a great power, it can hope to inflict costs on a great power out of proportion to what the great power can hope to gain by attacking it.[34]

The usage of the term 'middle power' is adapted from Wight's treatment of the subject. To avoid confusion, it is necessary to explain that Wight's standards or, at least, their qualifications are debatable. According to Wight, great powers have a tendency to "club together as a kind of directorate and impose their will on the states-system. They usually justify their actions as enforcing peace and security".[35] In 1919, great powers asserted at the Paris Peace Conference that they were the 'great responsibles' because they had wider interests and greater resources than the minor powers and, hence, a duty to police the world. The right of veto, accorded to various states in the League of Nations and subsequently in the United Nations Security Council, was taken as a sign of great power status.

'Middle-powerism' originated in the mid-1940s and was manifest in the policies of states at the San Francisco Conference in 1945. The great power status of the United States and the Soviet Union was not in dispute. The great power category was then a hardened category. The atomic bomb had nuclearized military strategy and frozen the international military structure. The middle power concept, as an attitude and as a policy, was, and remains, significant as a reaction to the world views of the two superpowers.

The extension of superpower competition into the Indian Ocean provides challenges and opportunities to the Indian Ocean middle powers to play the superpowers against each other, to improve the internal economic and military might of the middle powers; and to gradually transform the region into semi-autonomous units with some inherent strategic unity and a power structure. This appears to be the pattern of development in South Asia, the Middle East, and Southern Africa.

'Third-Worldism' is being promoted by the Indian Ocean states in contrast to superpowerism. In this regard, Horowitz refers to the "essential integrity and autonomy of the Third World".[36] This point deserves careful study because it is easy to regard post-1945 political and military relationships between Third World/Indian Ocean states and the superpowers in the framework of only two power blocs. The overt interstate relationships between Third World/Indian Ocean states and the United States and the Soviet Union obscures the deep hostility between the world views of the two superpowers and the Third World. The United States and the Soviet Union use different language but agree that international relations are essentially a struggle between two opposing systems. The Third World/ Indian Ocean states consider this neither a practical strategy nor the intellectual and moral basis of their foreign policy and military strategy.

Security in the Indian Ocean Area : Trends and Prospects

What are the present security trends in the Indian Ocean region? Do future prospects provide cause for optimism or pessimism? We shall attempt to provide tentative answers to these questions by analyzing the following dimensions of Indian Ocean security: general sources of tension and instability, recent superpower activities, specific regional disputes, and prospects for 'peace zone' or 'demilitarization' in the region.

General Sources of Tension and Instability

The Indian Ocean region manifests various symptoms of insecurity most of which are by no means restricted to that area but are present therein. They include the acquisition of conventional armaments from an ever-eager Soviet Union which has traditionally directed its arms supplies to the Middle East and Indian Ocean regions. Such militarization may contribute to the stability of specific regimes or maintain regional balances of military power. However, regimes stabilized by arms programmes may no longer be able to remain so. The pursuit of regional balance of power may lead to unending regional arms competitions. It is observed that no subregion of the Indian Ocean has remained immune to such adverse developments.

Likewise, the issue of nuclear proliferation has become firmly placed on Indian Ocean security agendas. Whether the prospect of increasing nuclearization in the Indian Ocean region contributes to insecurity is a debatable point. However, two contentious issues seem to be especially germane to a discussion on the Indian Ocean. First is the fear that the embryonic stage of national nuclear programmes may invite Osirak-style raids. Second is the view that a regional nuclear capacity would end the dependence of the Indian Ocean states on the superpowers and that such proliferation is necessary to induce serious arms control negotiations between the United States and the Soviet Union.

Another source of regional insecurity and instability can be seen in the extension of national jurisdiction over economic zones. At the very least, developments in the Law of the Sea and the need for policing new jurisdictions will certainly make additional demands on the navies of the littoral states.[37]

Finally, the above issues must be looked at in conjunction with the other persistent sources of conflict in the region. The problems of poverty, ethnic and religious divisions, seccessionism and internal political instabilities are characteristic of the Indian Ocean landscape.

Recent Super Power Activities

The recent policies of the Soviet Union and the United States in the Indian Ocean arena generated considerable concern in the world community. The Soviet policies in the Indian Ocean reflected the general trends in Soviet security in relation to Asia as a whole. This seemingly unending strategic interlinkages between the Middle East, the Persian Gulf, South Asia, the Sino-Soviet frontier, and the waters of the Indian Ocean present the USSR with something of a 'strategic seamless web'. Throughout the late 1970s a marked change was discernible in the Soviet Union's concept of security in the region, a drift from collective to selective patterns of Asian security. Its exclusion from the Middle East core, volatile Islamic movements in South-west Asia, renewed American military activities in the region, and Sino-American and Sino-Japanese pressures in South and East Asia made the Soviet plan of Indian Ocean security go hay-wire. Pravda highlighted Soviet misgivings when it referred on 9 April, 1979 to the 'defense line being created by the Pentagon along the Egypt-Israel-Persian Gulf-Diego Garcia-Australia perimeter.' It reflected the Soviet fear of an extended and 'integrated' threat to its security in the Indian Ocean region.

The invasion of Afghanistan was symptomatic of the disintegration of a Soviet 'grand design' for Asia. Just as Ethiopia could be wooed only at the cost of the 'loss' of Somalia, similarly the detente between Iran and Iraq, which Moscow had assiduously cultivated in the mid-1970s, also collapsed. Likewise, while the USSR would certainly prefer not to abandon relations with Pakistan, the latter's policies drove the two widely apart. Andrei Gromyko, while in Delhi in February 1980, complained publicly of Pakistan's negative and dangerous policies. It appeared that whatever preferred visions of Asian security it might have harboured, the Soviet Union responded to its regional security problems on ad hoc basis.

If the Soviet Union had a grand security design but seemed to have lost its way, then the United States appears only recently to have developed a coherent, active policy for the Indian Ocean. The Reagan administration saw "more geostrategic logic in viewing the Indian Ocean Basin as a strategic entity, linking together the littoral states of East Africa, the Arabian Peninsula, and South Asia".[38]

The 'ship-day' approach to the Indian Ocean security that dominated the Western political debate in the early 1970s is now not so obviously in vogue. This is partly a direct consequence of the increase in American naval activity in the ocean since 1979 and the decreased fear the USSR as the major naval intruder into the Indian Ocean waters. The shift of attention from counting ships reflects the fact that these naval presences are more a symptom of the security problem than the embodiment of it. This is not to deny the reality of these naval/military forces or the potential threat they might pose either to each other or to littoral states.

Regional Conflicts

Around the Indian Ocean, there are ongoing regional conflicts. Some of them are relatively quiescent; others have already erupted into fighting or threaten to do so imminently. Whether the over-all picture is better or worse than it was a decade ago is not, however, easy to discern.

Peace Zone and Demilitarization

Barry Buzan is probably correct in this 'negative' explanation for the persistence of the Indian Ocean zone-of-peace proposal in terms of which "the negotiations continue because nobody has any incentive to kill them off. The Non-Aligned have little to lose and something to gain by keeping them going. The Western powers and the USSR do not wish to attract the embarrassment and opprobrium of rejecting a regional arms control proposal out of hand".[39]

If the superpowers cannot reach some tacit agreement upon the nature and extent of their presence in the region, it is difficult to expect that the problem of accommodating the superpower relationship to a volatile Indian Ocean setting can even begin to be tackled. The Super Powers have a Janus-like quality, being both part of the problem and part of the solution.

REFERENCES

1. K. Waltz, *Theory of International Politics* (Reading, Mass.: Addison Wesley, 1979).
2. *Ibid.*, 2.
3. R. Keat and J. Urry, *Social Theory as Science* (London: Routledge and Kegan Paul, 1975).
4. T. Kuhn, *The Structure of Scientific Revolutions*, Second Edition (Chicago: University of Chicago Press, 1970), 23.
5. E.H. Carr, *The Twenty Years' Crisis* (London : Macmillan, 1939), (Quotations from the Second Edition, 1945).
6. H. Bull, 'The Theory of International Politics 1919-1969', in B. Porter (ed.), *The Aberystwyth Papers* (London : Oxford University Press, 1972), 35.
7. H. Morgenthau, *Politics Among Nations* (New York : Knopf, 1948) (all quotations are from the fifth edition, published in 1973).
8. Morgenthau, *op. cit.*, 3.
9. *Ibid.*, 4.
10. *Ibid.*, 5.
11. R. Snyder, H. Bruck and B. Sapin, *Foreign Policy Decision Making* (New York : Free Press, 1962).
12. M. Kaplan, *System and Process in International Politics* (New York : Wiley, 1957).
13. For Bull's original article, Kaplan's response, and a variety of other contributions, see K. Knorr and J. Rosenau (eds.), *Contending Approaches to International Politics* (Princeton, N.J.: Princeton University Press, 1969).
14. O. Young, 'Professor Russett : Industrious Tailor to a Naked Emperor', *World Politics*, Vol. 21 (1969), 486-511.

15. See the chapters by Job and Ostrom, Duvall and Starr, along with the rejoinder by Singer, in F. Hoole and D. Zinnes (eds.), Quantitative *International Politics* (New York : Praeger, 1976).
16. A. Buchan, *The End of the Postwar Era* (London : Weidenfeld and Nicolson, 1974).
17. S. Brown, *New Forces in World Politics* (Washington, D.C.:Brookings, 1974).
18. E. Morse, *Modernization and the Transformation of International Relations* (New York : Free Press, 1976), XVI.
19. *Ibid.*, 107.
20. R. Keohane and J. Nye, *Transnational Relations and World Politics* (Cambridge, Mass. : Harvard University Press, 1972).
21. R. Mansbach, Y. Ferguson and D. Lampert, *The Web of World Politics* (Englewood Cliffs, Mass. : Prentice-Hall, 1976).
22. R. Mansbach and J. Vasquez, *In Search of Theory* (New York : Columbia University Press, 1981).
23. Mansbach, Ferguson and Lampert, *op. cit.*, 276.
24. Michael Banks, "Systems Analysis and the Study of Regions", *International Studies Quarterly* 13, (December, 1969) : 343.
25. Donald C. Hellmann, "The Emergence of an East Asian International System", *International Studies Quarterly* 13 (December, 1969) : 423.
26. Leonard Binder, "The Middle East as a Subordinate International System", *World Politics* (April, 1958) : 408-29.
27. Michael Brecher, "International Relations and Asian Studies : The Subordinate State System of Southern Asia," *World Politics* 15 (January 1963) : 213-35. See also Brecher, *The New States of Asia* (London : Oxford University Press, 1963), and Brecher, "The Middle East Subordinate System and Its Impact on Israel's Foreign policy", *International Studies Quarterly* 13 (June 1969) : 117-39.
28. William Zartman, "Africa as a Subordinate State System in International Relations", *International Organization* 21 (Summer 1967) : 545-64.
29. Larry W. Bowman, "The Subordinate State System of Southern Africa", *International Studies Quarterly* 13 (September 1968) : 231-63.
30. Hellmann, "Emergence of an East Asian International System", 421-34.
31. Louis J. Cantori and Steven L. Spiegel, *The International Politics of Regions — A Comparative Approach* (Englewood Cliffs, N.J. : Prentice - Hall, 1970). See also Cantori and Spiegel, "International Regions : A Comparative Approach to Five Subordinate Systems", *International Studies Quarterly* 13 (December 1969) : 361-80, Cantori and Spiegel, "The International Politics of Re-

gions", *Polity* 2 (Summer 1970) : 397-425, and Cantori and Spiegel, "The Analysis of Regional International Politics : The Integration versus the Empirical Systems Approach", *International Organization* 27 (Autumn 1973) : 465-94.

32. Kenneth N. Waltz, *Theory of International Politics* (London : Addison - Wesley, 1979), 39.
33. Jawaharlal Nehru, *India's Foreign Policy : Selected Speeches*, 1946-61, p. 242.
34. Wight, *Power Politics*, pp. 63-65.
35. *Ibid.*, p. 42.
36. Irving L. Horowitz, *Beyond Empire and Revolution : Militarization and Consolidation in the Third World* (New York : Oxford University Press, 1982), p. vii.
37. Barry Buzan, "Naval Power, the Law of the Sea, and the Indian Ocean as a Zone of Peace", *Marine Policy* (July, 1981).
38. Sharin Tahir-Kheli and William O. Staudenmaier, "The Saudi-Pakistani Military Relationship : Implications for US Policy", *Orbis* (Spring 1982), p. 157.
39. Buzan, *Naval Power, the Law of the Sea, and the Indian Ocean*, p. 201.

CHAPTER II

Survey of Available Literature on the Indian Ocean

Review of available Literature

Since the end of the Second World War, the gradual liquidation of colonialism on the perimeter of the Indian Ocean has opened up a Pandora's Box of problems for the policy-makers in the various capitals of the world. For a century and a half, Great Britain held almost absolute sway over the area. The compulsions of the emerging political landscape left the British with no alternative but to withdraw gradually from the area. The multiple polities which replaced the British power in the area are faced with a host of chronic intra-state and inter-state problems. They are incapable of creating an international order in the area that may defeat the designs of outside Powers. It is important to remember that at no stage in the history of this area has any littoral country exercised dominant influence.

The literature on this subject is steadily growing. Our endeavour here is to make a survey of significant writings published in the English language (excluding the material published in the newspapers and news weeklies) mainly during the past quarter of a century on the problems arising from the situation developing in the Indian Ocean area. It may also be mentioned that only those books and articles which have an important and direct bearing on the subject have been chosen here.

In the category of the literature dealing with the historical background of the area, we may begin with comprehensive works such as Toussaint's *History of the Indian Ocean*,[1] Cox's *A Reference Guide to the Literature of Travel*,[2] Laird Clowe's *Sailing Ships*,[3] Philip's *Handbook of Oriental History*,[4] Wright and Platt's *Aid to Geographical Research*,[5] Ballard's *Rulers of the Indian Ocean*,[6] and Villier's *The Indian Ocean*.[7] Toussaint's book, originally written in French, is perhaps the best. It presents an excellent, though brief, history of the Indian Ocean covering a period of over twenty-five centuries. Ballard's is a pioneering effort and offers 'a continuous account of the special history of the sequence of periods of domination or ascendancy in the Indian Ocean held by various rival maritime states'. Villiers, who is the author of about a dozen books on the subject, writes with the authority of one who has sailed a good deal in and around the Ocean. The first few chapters of his book deal with the conditions of the Ocean. He then attempts a brief history of the area down to the end of the last world war.

Since the importance of the Indian Ocean territories has grown, some literature has been put out about their geography and history. Area Handbook for the Indian Ocean Territories[8] deals with the general character of the region, the Republic of Maldives, the colony of Seychelles and the British Indian Ocean Territory, Mauritius, and Reunion. Diego Garcia, a brief survey covering its geography, history, and politics, is a study made from the perspective of the littoral of the Indian Ocean.[9]

Apart from these general works, there are a few works written from the particular standpoint of India. Arthur Vincent's *The Defence of India*[10] and Victor Bayley's *Is India Impregnable?*[11] partly deal with India's maritime defence. Vincent devotes the first chapter of his book to a discussion of India's maritime defence in its international context as at the end of the First World War. In a very lucid enunciation and analysis, he discusses India's three naval bases, backyards, fuel resources, etc.[12] Bayley, who wrote on the eve of the Second World War, devotes Chapter 7 of his book to the 'Dangers from the sea'. However, in view of the recent advances in the methods and means of warfare made possible by scientific and technological developments, most of his views have become irrelevant.

By far the best work from India's standpoint is that of the

late K.M. Panikkar, whose books under different and yet related titles offer a penetrating insight into the different facets of the problems of the Indian Ocean area. The value of his contributions lies in the fact that he constantly keeps in view both the long, historical perspective and the complexities of contemporary problems and their implications for India. In this section we may confine ourselves to three of his books: *The Future of India and South-east Asia,*[13] *India and the Indian Ocean: An Essay on the Influence of Sea Power on Indian History,*[14] and *Geographical Factors in Indian History.*[15] The Future of India and South-East Asia deals with one region of the Indian Ocean area and pleads for a quadruple regional order with America, Britain, India, and Indonesia as its main pillars. The focus of India and the Indian Ocean is different. Here the author indicates how sea power influenced the course of Indian History from ancient times to the end of British rule in India. In the conclusion of the first edition of the book, and in Chapter VII and the conclusion of the second edition, he raised a few fundamental problems and offered some pragmatic suggestions. In *Geographical Factors in Indian History*, all kinds of factors are mentioned. It is pointed out that next to the Himalayas, the Indian Ocean has been the most decisive factor in the shaping of Indian history. Some of the points made in his earlier works are obviously restated though somewhat in a different manner.

Another work, D.E. Kennedy's *The Security of Southern Asia,*[16] deals with a very important region of the Indian Ocean area, namely the defence problems of the non-Communist countries of the area in the contest of Soviet and Chinese policies. It discusses the problems of a collective security system and also the role which the Western Powers and countries such as Australia should play in establishing such a system. Philip Allen's *Self-Determination in the Western Indian Ocean*[17] has the same theme in the context of another important region of the Indian Ocean.

Another kind of literature which constitutes an extremely significant part of the backdrop of the subject deals with the role of the sea in modern strategy. In the United States a large body of material has been brought out on the technical subject of military strategy. But not much attention has been given to the question of correlating national defence with international security. This gap is partly filled by L.W. Martin's *The Sea in Modern Strategy.*[18] Sponsored by the Institute for Strategic Studies, London, the book is a kind of link which joins the scarce naval literature with the literature on the wider problems of modern strategy. After discussing the various facets of the problem, the book reaches the conclusion that owing to the huge increase in the world's population, the expansion of economic activity, and the accompanying rise in the international interchange of goods and services, the use of the sea is bound to be intensified. Besides, the sea will become more important as a source of food and minerals. From the military point of view also the sea will continue to be of considerable political and strategic concern.

Multifoci

The Indian Ocean area has been a subject of study in books and monographs as well as in numerous research papers and articles, unmistakably indicating a growing sense of its importance. Perhaps the most significant organized pioneering effort to study the problem of the area was made in the early 1950s when, at the suggestion of the Institute of Pacific Relations, New York, the Indian Council of World Affairs set up a study group to look into 'the security and defence problems of the Indian Ocean area'. The upshot of this effort was the publication of a study under the title *Defence and Security in the Indian Ocean Area.*[19] Prepared in the international milieu of 1953-54, it covers practically every aspect of the problem: it deals with the geographical situation, economic and human factors, specific problems of the countries in the region, and, the interests of outside Powers. The factors that encourage major outside Powers to take interest in the area and which come in the way of creating a regional order are highlighted though, owing to political changes both at the regional and at the global levels, some of the conclusions of the study have lost their validity.

A book which gives partial attention to the interests and intentions of the various Powers is the second edition of *India and the Indian Ocean.*[20] It contains a new chapter which discusses the position of the Indian Ocean after the Second World War. In a summary exposition, Panikkar brings into sharp focus the political changes which were brought into being in the immediate post-war period. Similarly, Toussaint, in Chapter 15 of his book, entitled *Cancer and Capricorn*, touches upon recent developments.[21]

A significant exercise in studying the various facets of the problems facing the area was made at a conference organized by the Center for Strategic and International Studies of the Georgetown University in March 1971. A variety of papers, each representing the standpoint of a different country, were presented. A volume comprising these papers was published under the title *The Indian Ocean : Its Political, Economic and Strategic Importance.*[22] Beginning with trade, national resources, and strategy, it discusses the situation in the three main regions of the Indian Ocean area - the north-western approaches, the eastern ocean, and the western ocean. It concludes with an analysis of the interests and politics of the major Powers. It is a valuable book representing different perspectives. *The Indian Ocean and Threat to the West,*[23] edited by Patrick Wall, contains four studies in global strategy with reference to the Indian Ocean. It presents an exaggerated view of the threats to the West's security in this area. Adie's *Oil, Politics and Sea Power : The Indian Oceans Vortex*[24] is a monograph which examines the growing involvement of the Great Powers in the politics of the Indian Ocean area. It holds the view that any escalation in the area is likely to make it a theatre of conflict in a world already surfeited with all manner of problems. K. Rajendra Singh's *Politics of the Indian Ocean,*[25] *Indian Ocean Power Rivalry*[26] edited by T.T. Poulose, and Jagdish Vibhakar's *Afro-Asian Security and Indian Ocean*[27] also merit mention. The first of these books needs special attention as it attempts to correlate the evolution of the weapons system to the politics in this area. The second consists of papers of a seminar. Some of the pieces, as for instance Hedley Bull's, are really good. Devendra Kaushik's book is written in order "to correct the pro-Anglo-American stand usually adopted in studies on the problems of security in the Indian Ocean area".[28]

Recently the American Congress has held several hearings on the politics in the Indian Ocean area and related problems. These hearings have been published. They offer rich material reflecting the assessment of American scholars and officials of the policies of important littoral as well as outside Powers.

While some of the statements included in these publications lack adequate appreciation of the situation in the area, others present a balanced perspective. Two hearings have been directly on the subject. They are: The Indian Ocean, Political and Strategic Future[29] and Proposed Expansion of U.S. Military Facilities in the Indian Ocean.[30] Some other hearings on related areas are : U.S. Interests in and Policies Toward the Persian Gulf,[31] U.S. Interests in and Policies Toward South Asia,[32] and New Perspectives on the Persian Gulf.[33] Apart from these, another Congressional publication *Means of Measuring Naval Power* with Special Reference to US and Soviet Activities in the Indian Ocean[34] is helpful in studying those aspects of the naval development of the area about the importance of which there is no unanimity among analysts.

A report on the Indian Ocean Region published by the Australian Parliament's Joint Committee on Foreign Affairs offers valuable analysis. It discusses the role of important states — outside as well as littoral — in the area.[35] Australia being the vantage point of the report, some of the presumptions of the study and the conclusions presented in it are of doubtful validity for other littoral states. Another report of the Conference entitled Economic and Political Development in Relation to Sea Power Along the Routes from the Indian Ocean[36] presents the standpoint essentially of the West. The Conference was held in London in May 1972 and was attended by some Asian scholars also. The Soviet position in the Indian Ocean is blown out of proportions and the littoral sentiment is more or less ignored. A issue of Seminar[37] is also exclusively devoted to the Indian Ocean and contains a fair analysis of the various facets of the problem.

When we pass on to the periodical literature, reference may be made to Maharaj K. Chopra's paper "Indian Ocean Strategy".[38] Not only did the author indicate the importance of the location of the Indian Ocean, of the islands in the Ocean, of the long distances that separate them, but he also briefly discussed the international political situation as it obtained in the area.

For understandable reasons, the Royal Institute of International Affairs, London, caused a few significant studies to be prepared, and published them in a special issue of the

International Affairs entitled "Britain East of Suez".[39] The contributors included well-known scholars who offered studies from different vantage points.[40] The British, American, Commonwealth, Southeast Asian, Australian, and Chinese viewpoints were all taken into account. Surprisingly, no study that represented the attitude of the Soviet Union was included. It is much less surprising that the Institute did not attach much importance to the attitude of India or of other important littoral states.

On the eve of the British withdrawal from the Indian Ocean area, a distinguished Indian, V.T. Krishnamachari, wrote his brief note entitled 'Regional Arrangements: The Indian Ocean Area'. This was one of the earliest to appear on the subject.[41] Krishnamachari sought to identify the main problem and urged that, under Articles 52-54 of the UN Charter, a regional arrangement comprising all countries in the region should be brought into being. He pleaded for the establishment of a defence council and an economic council for the region. Considering the context in which he wrote the note, it is no wonder that he was not to anticipate the subsequent trends in international and regional politics. With the advantage of hindsight, we may say that he took an oversimplified view of the situation. Recently, a few other Indian scholars have given attention to the various problems of this area. Almost all of them have considered the interference of outside Powers as undesirable and pleaded for some sort of a regional order in which the littoral states play the main role. Some of the more significant writings in the category include K. Subrahmanyam and J.P. Anand, "Indian Ocean as an Area of Peace",[42] A.P.S. Bindra, "The Indian Ocean as seen by an Indian",[43] and K.P. Misra's two articles entitled "Afro-Asian Ocean"[44] and "International Politics in the Indian Ocean".[45]

Another essay, Allen's 'Self-Determination in the Western Indian Ocean', is also valuable.[46] Confining himself to the western part of the area which, with the exception of southern Africa, mostly consists of small islands and islets scattered all over the Ocean, the author envisages a major role for the United Nations in relation to these territories. He suggests 'a regional solution protected by multilateral activity'. Dieter Braun's 'The Indian Ocean in Afro-Asian Perspective' takes a fairly realistic position when it warns the Great Powers that if they fail to take into account the aspirations of the littoral states and seek to achieve their aims through traditional strategies, they are not likely to succeed.[47] Diethlem Weidemann's article 'Imperialist Bases in the Indian Ocean' considers bases established by the Western Powers as a source of international tensions and as a threat to the independent development of littoral states.[48] Of the two pieces by D.C. Watt, "The Decision to Withdraw from the Gulf"[49] and "British and the Indian Ocean: Diplomacy before Defence",[50] the latter is more significant in that it urges the British government to try for the neutralization of the area through international organizations, a scheme which would also mean 'agreed withdrawal of all non-littoral naval vessels from the Indian Ocean area'. Contrary to this view, Alvin J. Cottrell and R.M. Burrell's 'No Power Can hope to Dominate the Indian Ocean' considers the neutralization solution a mere will-o'-the-wisp and highlights the implications of the closure of the Suez Canal.[51]

Some articles which are less significant but which address themselves to the general theme are Ramesh Dutta Dikshit's "Maldive Islands: The Harbinger of Cold War in the Indian Realm",[52] Bishwanath Singh's "The Oceanic and Their Potential for the Andamans and Nicobar Islands,"[53] Anthony Harrigan's "The Afro-Asian Ocean World",[54] Moleworth's "Some Problems of Future Security in the Indian Ocean Area",[55] Ratsimbazafy's "The Indian Ocean: New Strategic Role"[56] and "Positive Neutralism: New Balance in the Indian Ocean"[57] Ravindra Varma's "Power and Politics in the Indian Ocean",[58] Millar's "Control of the Indian Ocean",[59] Jayaraman's "Symposium on the Indian Ocean"[60] Furlong's "Strategic Powers in the Indian Ocean",[61] Simon's "A Systems Approach to Security in the Indian Ocean Arc",[62] Thompson's "Problems in the Indian Ocean",[63] Ganon's "Military Consideration in the Indian Ocean",[64] McConnell and Kelly's "Super Power Naval Diplomacy in the Indo-Pakistani Crisis",[65] and Kaul's "The Indo-Pakistan War and the Changing Balance of Power in the Indian Ocean".[66]

Relevant parts of the three SIPRI World Armament and Disarmament Yearbooks also deal with problems of the area.[67] These volumes offer fairly objective and neat treatment of the subject. Some literature on the arms limitation in the area has also appeared. Barnds' "Arms Race or Arms Control in the Indian Ocean"[68] and Wriggins' "Heading Off a New Arms Race : Let's Try to Neutralize the Indian Ocean"[69] offer constructive ideas.

Zone of Peace

Since the Twenty-sixth Session (1971) of the U.N. General Assembly, substantial literature has come out on the establishment of zone of peace in the Indian Ocean. This material is very useful because it not only discusses the various phases and facets of the concept of zone of peace, but also throws light on the policies of the member-countries of the U.N. towards an international order in this area.

The U.N. material can be classified into two parts—the debates which reveal the opinions of individual countries and some documents prepared by the committees working under the auspices of the U.N. Beginning with the Twenty-sixth Session, the subject was under consideration during four Sessions of the Assembly. Most of these debates took place in the meetings of the First Committee. It is a rich source material for researchers on the subject and encompasses the arguments for as well as against the zone of peace proposal. The implications of the proposal are well brought out in the speeches of the representative of Sri Lanka. Among the major documents, two reports of the Ad Hoc Committee on the Indian Ocean[70] and two statements prepared by the experts appointed by the Secretary-General are significant. Apart from a brief resume of the work of the Ad Hoc Committee, its first report consists of a working paper by Sri Lanka, excerpts from statements made in the Committee, and a statement by Amarasinghe. The second report also presents a review of the work of the Committee, and has a few recommendations. In so far as the statements by experts are concerned, they were prepared pursuant to the General Assembly resolution 3080 (xxviii).[71] The first statement contains a description of the military and naval presence and deployment of outside Powers in the Indian Ocean and factors contributing to a potential arms race. This statement was criticized by many and hence the Secretary-General ordered that the statement be reviewed in the light of the observations made by various countries. Consequently, the second statement was issued replacing the first. To this list of U.N. material, four resolutions passed by the U.N. General Assembly

may also be added.[72] Of these, the first enunciating the principle of peace zone was substantive in nature while the other three were procedural.

India's Problems and Tasks

It is needless to emphasise the point that for India the Indian Ocean and the area surrounding it are immensely important. In itself it may not be significant for India that the Ocean is named after it, but certain facts — its location, size, population (about half of the population of the area resides in India), power potential, etc., as compared with those of the other countries of the area — make its concern in the area acute.

It is, therefore, natural that several Indian scholars, and a few foreign ones too, should write books and articles on the subject in its historical as well as contemporary setting. Among them the name of K.M. Panikkar stands out. In the Future of India and Southeast Asia he makes a plea for some kind of a collective security system comprising "all powers directly concerned with sharing in responsibility".[73] His main argument is that "a free and stable government in India conscious of its responsibility and capable of playing its part in Southeast Asia is the essential pre-requisite of the success of any such scheme".[74] In another book entitled *India and the Indian Ocean*, he devotes his attention exclusively to India's role in the area. After stating all the foreseeable problems of the post-war period and emphasizing India's role in their context, he makes several suggestions in order to make India's role effective. In his last work on the subject, *Problems of Indian Defence,*[75] he deals in general with India's naval preparedness. The problems of naval defence from India's standpoint are also examined in K.B. Vaidya's *The Naval Defence of India.*[76] The author regrets India's indifference in the early years of its independence to the development of naval power and pleads for vigorous efforts to make up for the lost time. K. Sridharan's *A Maritime History of India,* though essentially a non-political study, is useful inasmuch as its describes the growth of the Indian Navy, which has its own political and security implications.[77] In Defence and Security in the Indian Ocean Area, India's interests are identified. The study says that "to India, the security of this region is of paramount importance as oceanic routes across this Ocean carry the bulk of her overseas trade".[78] A point which this study makes is that "the interests and powers outside the region in the security of the area are such that the nations of the region are not quite free to decide their security policies according to their interests and resources".[79]

Besides these books, there are a good number of scholarly papers and articles on India and the area. On the eve of India's independence, the problem of ensuring its security after the British withdrawal from the country became important and some scholars gave thought to the nature of the problem and its possible solutions. K.M. Panikkar's "The Defence of India and Indo-British Obligations"[80] and V.T. Krishnamachari's "Regional Arrangement : The Indian Ocean Area"[81] are two of the best instances of such an effort. Both suggested India and British playing a role in the area could not naturally anticipate the turn which events in the area took in future. Several aspects of the multi-dimensional problems of the area are described and analysed in a series of articles published from time to time in the *Journal of the United Service Institute of India.* Here mention may be made of W.E. Parry's "Indian and Sea Power",[82] V.A. Kamath's "India and Sea Power",[83] C.S. Venkatachar's "Influence of Sea Power in the Indian ocean",[84] Narpati Datta's "An Aircraft Carrier for the Indian Navy",[85] N. Krishnan's "A Strategic Concept of India's Naval Expansion",[86] "India Can Ignore Her Navy Only at Her Peril" by "Fremen",[87] Har Prasad's "India : An Old Maritime Power",[88] B.B. Basu's "Military Evaluation of Seas and Oceans and the Geographical Bases of Sea Power",[89] and K. Subrahmanyam's "Ebb and Flow of Power in the Indian Ocean Area".[90] A piece prepared by a Naval Study Group, "Power Vacuum in the Indian Ocean", makes out a strong case for strengthening India's naval capability.[91]

Anthony Harrigan points out the possible dangers to India from the Ocean side, mainly in the context of the activities of countries such as China, Indonesia, and the Soviet Union.[92] Indicating the growth of the Indian Navy, the author highlights the importance of the Indian Ocean for India by approvingly quoting Panikkar's words: "Whoever controls the Indian Ocean has India at his mercy."

REFERENCES

1. Auguste Toussaint, *History of the Indian Ocean,* June Guicharnaud, trans., (London, 1966).
2. E.C. Cox, *A Reference Guide to the Literature of Travel* (Washington, D.C., 1935), 2 Vols.
3. C.S.L. Laird Clowes, *Sailing Ships* : Their History and Development as Illustrated by the Collection of Ship-models in the Science Museum (London, 1952), 2 Vols., edn. 4.
4. C.H. Philips, ed., *Handbook of Oriental History* (London, 1950).
5. J.K. Wright and E.T. Platt, *Aids to Geographical Research* (New York, 1947).
6. G.A. Ballard, *Rulers of the Indian Ocean* (New York, N.Y., 1947).
7. Alan Villiers, *The Indian Ocean* (London, 1922).
8. Area Handbook for the Indian Ocean Territories, Prepared for the American University by the Institute for Cross-Cultural Research (Washington, D.C., 1971).
9. Diego Garcia, Parliamentary Research and Information Service, Lok Sabha Secretariat (New Delhi, 1974).
10. Arthur Vincent, *The Defence of India* (London, 1922).
11. Victor Bayley, *Is India Impregnable?* (London)
12. Arthur Vincent, *op. cit.*, p. 6.
13. K.M. Panikkar, *The Future of India and South-East Asia* (London, 1943).
14. *India and the Indian Ocean* : An Essay on the Influence of Sea Power on Indian History (London, 1951).
15. *Geographical Factors in Indian History* (Bombay, 1959).
16. D.E. Kennedy, The Security of Southern Asia (London, 1965).
17. Philip M. Allen, Self-Determination in the Western Indian Ocean (New York, 1966), *International Conciliation No. 560*.
18. L.W. Martin, *The Sea in Modern Strategy* (London, 1965).
19. Indian Council of World Affairs, *Defence and Security in the Indian Ocean Area* (Bombay, 1958).
20. Panikkar, n. 14.
21. See Toussaint, n. 1.
22. Alvin J. Cottrell and R.M. Burrell (eds.), *The Indian Ocean : Its Political, Economic and Military Importance* (New York, 1972).
23. Patrik Wall (ed.), *The Indian Ocean and Threat to the West* (London, 1975).
24. W.A.C. Adie, *Oil, Politics and Sea Power : The Indian Ocean Vortex* (New York, 1975).
25. K. Rajendra Singh, *Politics of the Indian Ocean* (New Delhi, 1974).
26. T.T. Poulose (ed.), *Indian Ocean Power Rivalry* (New Delhi, 1974).
27. Jagdish Vibhakar, *Afro-Asian Security and Indian Ocean* (New Delhi, 1974).
28. Devendra Kaushik, *The Indian Ocean : Towards a Peace Zone* (New Delhi, 1972).

29. *The Indian Ocean : Political and Strategic Future* (Washington, 1971).
30. *Proposed Expansion of U.S. Military Facilities in the Indian Ocean* (Washington, 1974).
31. *U.S. Interests in and Policies Toward the Persian Gulf* (Washington, 1972).
32. *U.S. Interests in and Policies Toward South Asia* (Washington, 1973).
33. *New Perspectives on the Persian Gulf* (Washington, 1973)
34. *Means of Measuring Naval Power with Special Reference to U.S. and Soviet Activities in the Indian Ocean* (Washington, 1974).
35. Indian Ocean Region : Report from the Joint Committee on Foreign Affairs, 1971 (Canberra, 1972), Parliamentary Paper 258.
36. Economic and Political Development in Relation to Sea Power Along the Routes from the Indian Ocean (New York, 1972). The Conference was organized by the New York University and the National Strategy Information Center, New York.
37. Seminar (New Delhi), No. 181 (September, 1974).
38. Maharaj K. Chopra, 'Indian Ocean Strategy', *Military Review* (Fort Leavenworth, Kans.), May, 1965, pp. 85-95.
39. *International Affairs* (London), Vol. 42, April, 1966.
40. The Studies included in the special issue are: Michael Howard, 'Britain's Strategic Problem East of Suez'; Alastair Buchan, 'Britain in the Indian Ocean'; George K. Tanham, 'A United States View'; Maurice Zinkin, 'The Commonwealth and Britain East of Suez'; J.D.B. Miller, 'An Australian View'; W.A.C. Adie, 'Some Chinese Attitudes'; and Hugh Hanning, 'Britain East of Suez : Facts and Figures'.
41. V.T. Krishnamachari, 'Regional Arrangements : The Indian Ocean Area', *India Quarterly* (New Delhi), Vol. 2 (1946), pp. 287-89.
42. K. Subrahmanyam and J.P. Anand, *'Indian Ocean as an Area of Peace'*, Vol. 27 (1971), pp. 289-315.
43. A.P.S. Bindra, 'The Indian Ocean as Seen by an Indian', *Proceedings of the U.S. Naval Institute* (Annapolis, Md.), May, 1970, pp. 178-203.
44. K.P. Misra, 'Afro-Asian Ocean', *Seminar* (New Delhi), October, 1971, pp. 31-35.
45. K.P. Misra, 'International Politics in the Indian Ocean', *Orbis,* Vol. XVIII, Number 4 (Winter, 1975), pp. 1088-1108.
46. Philip M. Allen, 'Self-Determination in the Western Indian Ocean', *International Conciliation* (New York, N.Y.), No. 560, November, 1966, pp. 1-74.
47. Dieter Braun 'The Indian Ocean in Afro-Asian Perspective', *World Today* (London), June, 1972, pp. 249-256.
48. Diethlem Weidemann, 'Imperialist Bases in the Indian Ocean', *United Asia* (Bombay), Vol. 23 (1971), pp. 372-382.

49. D.C. Watt, 'The Decision to Withdraw from the Gulf', *Political Quarterly* (London), Vol. 39 (1968), pp. 301-321.
50. Idem, 'Britain and the Indian Ocean: Diplomacy Before Defence', *Ibid.*, Vol. 42 (1971), pp. 306-315.
51. Alvin J. Cottrell and R.M. Burrell, 'No Power Can Hope to Dominate the Indian Ocean', *New Middle East* (London), September, 1971, pp. 35-37.
52. Ramesh Dutta Dikshit, 'Maldives Islands : The Harbinger of Cold War in the Indian Realm : A Study in Political Geography', *Modern Review* (Calcutta), November, 1963, pp. 362-365.
53. Bishwanath Singh, 'The Oceanic and Their Potential for the Andamans and Nicobar Islands', *Ibid.*, April, 1968, pp. 232-235.
54. Anthony Harrigan, 'The Afro-Asian Ocean World', *Proceedings of the U.S. Naval Institute*, May, 1965, pp. 44-59.
55. G.N. Molesworth, 'Some Problems of Future Security in the Indian Ocean Area', *Asiatic Review* (London), January, 1946, pp. 44-59.
56. A Ratsimbazafy, 'The Indian Ocean : New Strategic Role', *Review of International Affairs* (Belgrade), 20 October, 1967, pp. 18-19.
57. Idem, 'Positive Neutralism : New Balance in the Indian Ocean', *Ibid.*, 20 May, 1969, pp. 11-12.
58. Ravindra Varma, 'Power and Politics in the Indian Ocean', *Foreign Affairs Report* (New Delhi), January, 1964, pp. 3-6.
59. T.B. Millar, 'Control of Indian Ocean', *Ibid.*, January, 1968, pp. 1-4. Also see his 'The Indian and Pacific Oceans : Some Strategic Considerations', *Adelphi Papers* (London), No. 57 (1969).
60. R. Jayaraman, 'Symposium on Indian Ocean', *Journal of Scientific and Industrial Research* (New Delhi), Vol. 26, pp. 190-195.
61. R.D.M. Furlong, 'Strategic Powers in the Indian Ocean', *International Defence Review* (Geneva), Vol. 5 (April, 1972).
62. S.W. Simon, 'A Systems Approach to Security in the Indian Ocean Arc', *Orbis* (Philadelphia), Vol. 14 (Summer, 1970). pp. 401-442.
63. George G. Thompson, 'Problems in the Indian Ocean', *Pacific Community* (Tokyo), Vol. 3 (October, 1971), pp. 126-141.
64. Edmund Joseph Ganon, 'Military Consideration in the Indian Ocean', *Current History* (Philadelphia), November, 1972, pp. 218-221.
65. James M. McConnell and Anne M. Kelly, 'Super Power Naval Diplomacy in the Indo-Pakistani Crisis', *Professional Paper* No. 108 (February, 1973), Center for Naval Analysis, Arlinon, Va.
66. Lieutenant Commander Ravi Kaul (Retd.) 'The Indo-Pakistan War and the Changing Balance of Power in the Indian Ocean', U.S. Naval Institute Proceedings, *Naval Review*, 1973, pp. 174-195.
67. *SIPRI*, World Armament and Disarmament Yearbook (Stockholm), 1972, 1973, 1974.
68. William J. Barnds, 'Arms Race or Arms Control in the Indian Ocean', *America*, Vol. 127 (October, 1972), pp. 280-282.

69. Howard Wriggins, 'Heading Off a New Arms Race : Let's Try to Neutralize the Indian Ocean', *War/Peace Report* (New York), Vol. II (August-September, 1971), pp. 7-11.
70. UNGA, Official Records, Twenty-eighth Session Supplement No. 29 (A/9029), and UNGA, Official Records, Twenty-ninth Session, Supplement No. 29 (*/9629).
71. UN Doc. A/AC. 159/1, 3 May, 1974, and UN Doc. A/AC. 159/1/Rev. I, II July, 1974.
72. The four resolutions are documented as follows:
(a) A/Res./2832 (XXVI), 16 December, 1971.
(b) A/Res./2992 (XXVII), 9 January, 1973.
(c) A/Res./3080 (XXVIII), 19 December, 1973.
(d) A/Res./9905 (XXIX), 5 December, 1974.
73. K.M. Panikkar, *Future of India and Southeast Asia,* p. 17.
74. *Ibid.*
75. K.M. Panikkar, *Problems of Indian Defence* (Bombay, 1960).
76. K.B. Vaidya, *The Naval Defence of India* (Bombay, 1949).
77. K. Sridharan, *A Maritime History of India* (Delhi, 1965).
78. *Defence and Security in the Indian Ocean Area,* n. 19, p. viii.
79. *Ibid.,* p. 184.
80. K.M. Panikkar, 'The Defence of India and Indo-British Obligations', *International Affairs* (London), Vol. 22, January, 1946, pp. 85-90.
81. Krishnamachari, n. 40.
82. W.E. Parry, 'India and Sea Power', *U.S.I. Journal* (New Delhi), January-March, 1949, pp. 17-27.
83. *Ibid.,* January-March, 1954, pp. 78-85.
84. *Ibid.,* July-October, 1953, pp. 153-163.
85. *Ibid.,* April-June, 1957, pp. 113-115.
86. *Ibid.,* April-June, 1957, pp. 212-222.
87. *Ibid.,* October-December, 1963, pp. 321-328.
88. *Ibid.,* October-December, 1967, pp. 335-340.
89. *Ibid.,* October-December, 1967, pp. 335-357.
90. *Ibid.,* January-March, 1968, pp. 3-14.
91. 'Power Vacuum in the Indian Ocean', *The Hamla* (Bombay), November, 1968, pp. 34-42.
92. Anthony Harrigan, 'India's Maritime Posture', *Military Review,* Vol. 49, April, 1969, pp. 24-30.

CHAPTER III

Super Power Interests in the Indian Ocean Region

Political Objectives

The US interests that have determined the US policies in the Indian Ocean stem from the relevance of resources and geopolitics of the region to the worldwide balance of power. In this sense, the US interests in this area are directly linked with her security interests in Europe and East Asia because of the dependence of her allies on the Persian Gulf oil. The US interests in this region may be stated as follows: (1) to ensure access to secure oil supplies at reasonable prices; (2) to balance the Soviet presence, and, if possible to reduce the Soviet influence; (3) to promote stability and peaceful change on the domestic political and regional level; and (4) to pursue regional security and advance the Middle East peace process, while guaranteeing the security of Israel.[1]

The US political interests relate to two important goals. First is the objective of limiting the Soviet influence, or undermining it wherever possible. Historically, the Indian Ocean region has been under Western influence. But the Soviet third world diplomacy aiming to weaken this traditional influence through a combination of diplomatic, economic and military instruments has generated fears of domination. The attempts of the Soviet leadership to expand influence in the Indian Ocean region is seen by the U.S. and her regional allies as a destabilising factor, and thus a threat to the U.S. interests. The concern about the Soviet pressures which are generally psychological and a spectre of its grand geopolitical design for the region, has continuously raised questions about the U.S. stakes. The pro-

West regional states have, in particular, shown interest in the U.S. role to balance the Soviet moves. The U.S. declaratory policy addresses the fears of regional allies and has responded by augmenting her capabilities in contingencies. While in the security sense the U.S. presence in the area serves the purposes of deterrence, politically it not only reassures her allies of her interest in their territorial integrity but also signifies her commitments.

The second political objective centres around the notion of stability which might be identified with political tranquility in friendly states and intra-regional balance or with peaceful political change both domestically and in inter-state relations. The U.S. policy-makers have taken a realistic or pragmatic view of political order in third world societies. In other words, despite adherence to democratic ideals at home, authoritarianism is acceptable overseas as long as the political interests of the ruling establishments in third world countries are congruous with the U.S. policy objectives.

Security Interests

The U.S. security interests in the Indian Ocean are interlinked with her security interests in other important regions of the world. The security networks developed by the U.S. in the Indian Ocean, though designed to ensure regional security interests, are capable of supporting the U.S. strategic objectives in the Pacific and the Mediterranean. It is reasonable to assume that superpower conflict in any strategic region would escalate horizontally to other important areas because either side would be tempted to open up new fronts in order to stretch the forces of its adversary.

The U.S. force structure and facilities have been constructed to achieve two identical but mutually reinforcing security objectives. First, security against the Soviet pressures. In this regard, U.S. security concerns have corresponded with the fears and sensitivities of pro-West regimes. The second objective relates to security against a variety of regional threats ranging from domestic turmoil in a friendly country to intra-regional conflict which threatens the security of friendly states.

In the context of sea-based strategic planning, the Indian Ocean provides great potential for U.S. deterrence against the Soviet Union. The maintenance of a healthy balance and a credible deterrence in the area are the basic principles of the U.S. policy. The Indian Ocean, for American submarine purposes, has many advantages over other areas of strategic deployment, as many targets on the Soviet territory are accessible from the Bay of Bengal or the Arabian Sea.[2] Since 1960, the U.S. Navy has opted for a full-scale undersea long-range missile programme for the advantages of mobility and lesser vulnerability.[3] As landbased missiles have become increasingly vulnerable due to the accuracy and first-strike capability attained by the Soviet Union, undersea offensive and defensive systems have become pivotal to the U.S. strategic considerations.

Apart from a global strategic dimension, the U.S. security interests in the Indian Ocean relate to two additional objectives. First is the safeguarding of the Sea Lanes of Communications (SLOCs). In peace time, routine U.S. deployments in the Indian Ocean with periodic augmentation by carrier battle groups, are intended to demonstrate the capability to keep the SLOCs open to the oil and commercial traffic of the Western alliance. Any interruption in the supply of oil by the local powers through the Bab el Mandeb Straits at the mouth of the Red Sea or the Straits of Hormuz at the end of the Persian Gulf would be met with the use of the U.S. forces in the area. The Iranian threat to close the Strait of Hormuz as a retaliation against Iraqi attacks on third-party shipping taking oil from Iran's facilities was rebuffed by the U.S. declaration that she had the power and resolve to keep the straits open, using force if necessary. Although the United States has developed a clear margin of maritime superiority to deter attacks against SLOCs, the combat situations, particularly those involving the regional states, make it difficult for U.S. to use force. The persistent Iraqi attacks against third-party ships suspected of carrying Iranian oil are a case in point. The U.S. began to show concern only when Iran retaliated against ships taking oil from GCC countries.

The second US objective is to ensure the security of friendly regional states which complement the U.S. security interests. After the Soviet intervention in Afghanistan and the revolution in Iran, security assistance to the pro-West regional states has become the central concern of the U.S. policy. The 1979 crises in South-west Asia had adverse effects on the U.S. credibility to stabilise the region. The pro-West states in the Gulf began to reassess their security links with the United States because of the perceived risks of such a relationship. Therefore, since the early 1980s, the U.S. has launched a massive programme of security assistance to friendly regional states, including modernisation. The security co-operation includes not only transfer of the U.S. and the Western equipment, but also training of local armed forces and sharing of surveillance and intelligence.

Economic Interests

Oil is the life blood of modern industrial societies. Scme 60 per cent of the world's imported petroleum comes from the Persian Gulf region. There is no doubt that the total loss of this oil to the economies of the West and the industrialised Far East would be a blow of catastrophic proportions. The importance of Middle East oil by itself is very marginal to the U.S. requirements. The United States has significantly reduced oil imports from the Gulf to 1.4 million barrels a day. By adopting conservation measures alone, the United States cut down her oil consumption in the early 1980s by almost 2.8 million barrels a day. But the loss of supplies from that region would cause irreparable damage to the U.S. allies which it would be difficult to compensate for from other sources.

The current trend in the international oil market suggests that oil demand may continue to be weak because of the recession in the world economy and new and effective energy saving measures. Besides, the over-production by the Oil and Petroleum Exporting Countries (OPEC) has created an oil glut. Frequent attacks on neutral shipping in the Gulf war and a significant reduction in the oil exports of Iran and Iraq have not produced an oil crisis. It is estimated that there is unutilised petroleum production capacity of at least 8 million barrels a day, which is equal to roughly 15 per cent of current world usage. About one-third of this capacity is understood to be outside of the South-West Asian region, which would sufficiently compensate for even the total loss of oil from Iran and Iraq. It is also a fact that neither Iran nor Iraq has the military capability to close the

Gulf. However, the psychological repercussions of an interdiction of oil traffic by the belligerents will be construed as a challenge to the U.S. for her commitments to keep the oil flow from the Gulf open.

In addition to the energy security of the allies, ttÿÿÿheÿhe U.S. multi-national corporations have substantial capital investments in the Persian Gulf oil production, transportation and sale in the world market. The oil-producing areas of South-West Asia, with a petrodollar boom and ambitious development plans, have become a multi-billion dollar market for the manufactured goods of Japan, Western Europe and the United States. In 1981, the U.S. exported almost $11 billion in goods to the Gulf region alone, which is about 5 per cent of American exports worldwide.[4]

America's large-scale transfer of conventional arms to the Indian Ocean region is also a matter of great economic interest. Arms sales by the United States to Third World countries grew from less than a billion dollars in 1970 to approximately $11.2 billion in 1977.[5] Arms transfers are rationalised as an instrument of diplomatic, military and economic policy. In recent years the Middle East/Persian Gulf region has become the focus of arms flow. In FY 1974, Iran, Israel and Saudi Arabia accounted for 82 per cent of all arms ordered through the U.S. Foreign Military Sales Programme. In the same year, these three countries agreed to purchase nearly nine billion dollars of American arms. This trend has continued in the region, except for Iran, since the Islamic revolution. Egypt, Israel and Saudi Arabia have alone purchased U.S. arms worth nine and a half billion dollars between 1978-82.[6] The volume of military sales agreements and the transfer of advanced weapons to friendly states in the Indian Ocean region indicate the rising economic and security stakes of the U.S. and her allies.

Apart from the issues of energy and security, the U.S. dependence on foreign sources of minerals which are essential to industry and defence has increased. Many of the important minerals are imported from the most volatile areas of the world, thereby raising fears of the disruption of supplies. The U.S. lists 35 materials as strategic and it depends heavily on imports from other countries for 23 of them.

At a hearing before the House Subcommittee on Mines and Mining, Alexander Haig, then the Secretary of State, warned of a potential 'resource war'.[7] It was feared that instability and conflict in African countries might endanger the supply of strategic minerals to the industrial core. Compared with the American dependency, the Soviets obtain their supplies of critical minerals, mainly from Warsaw Pact countries. The Soviet Union is almost self-sufficient in strategic minerals, except for aluminium, flourine and tungsten.[8] In order to ensure continued access to the strategic resources of Africa and Asia, the American policy-makers have favoured an augmented Indian Ocean presence.

Analysis of Threat Perceptions

At present, Western powers control most of the egress and ingress points to the Indian Ocean and, in a conflict situation, reinforcement for the Soviet ships in the area would be extremely difficult. The U.S. 7th Fleet dominates the Western Pacific and Eastern approaches to the Indian Ocean. In time of war, the Soviet ships would be isolated in the Indian Ocean without shore-based air protection and would be extremely vulnerable to NATO forces.

It is a fact that the Soviet Union is itself becoming increasingly dependent on maritime trade and commerce. Any Soviet attempt to disrupt Western commerce and shipping would make Soviet naval units 'hostages' elsewhere.[9] The Soviet Union would perhaps refrain from threatening the oil and sea lanes of the area in peacetime and might take advantage of Western vulnerabilities in terms of distances and logistical problems only in wartime.

At present, threats to the U.S. interests might be seen as emanating less from a Soviet naval presence than revolutionary wars and intra-state conflicts. After the revolution in Iran, the strength of Islamic fundamentalism has grown rapidly. The revolutionary momentum of fundamentalism is largely a response to the arbitrary and authoritarian rule of dynastic elites in South-West Asia who are perceived as the middlemen of Western domination. The low-intensity conflicts that often result from the revolutionary movements can hardly be fought by the kind of superior forces which the United States has the capacity to mobilise. Although political threats to the stability of pro-West elites exist, they would not inevitably lead to successful revolutions. But if internal revolutions cause political upheavals, the United States would have only limited means to influence events.

In recent years an insurgent Iran and its Islamic fundamentalism have posed a serious challenge to the security of the Gulf region. The rulers of the Gulf states fear Iranian-inspired subversion. Concern about revolutionary Iran's intentions in the region intensified in December 1981 with an alleged Tehran-backed attempt to provoke chaos and presumably overthrow the ruling Khalifa family in Baharain.[10] The eagerness of some of the Ayatollahs in Iran to export their Islamic revolution to the Gulf countries tended to draw those countries together through the Gulf Co-operation Council and pushed them steadily towards the United States. The GCC countries gradually changed their attitude towards the U.S. military presence and access to Oman and even began to value an American connection despite considerable risks from militantly anti-American Arab states and movements. The United States shares the concern of friendly South-West Asian states about internal subversion. However, the United States would prefer to help the regional states to help themselves by providing security assistance and logistics support.

The intra-regional conflict such as the Iran-Iraq war has the potential to escalate to other states. Where adjacent states fail to maintain a neutral position and involve themselves indirectly, they become tempting targets, especially those which are weak and vulnerable. The option of the GCC countries to support Iraq was a strategic compulsion, because defeat of Iraq would not only change the balance of power in the Gulf but would also dangerously expose the entire region to the Iranian political and military assaults. The GCC's financial backing of Iraq, which is quite substantial, has on occasion caused retaliation from Iran. Iran attacked tankers of Kuwait and Saudi Arabia in May 1984. In the early stages of the war, it bombed Kuwaiti oil facilities along the border with Iraq. And in June, Saudis downed two intruding Iranian jets close to Saudi waters.

These events show the tendency of a regional conflict to explode into a larger conflagration.

Soviet Ideology and Third World Diplomacy

Lenin's support for the liberation of colonial areas and the linkages he emphasised at the 1920 Conference of the Comintern between the revolutionary struggle of the working class and the situation of oppressed colonial peoples might be considered the first attempt at a global Soviet role in the third world. The Bolsheviks fully realised the economic and strategic importance of the adjacent Indian Ocean littoral regions where anti-imperialist movements were gaining strength. Lenin recognised the decisive importance of the South-Asian subcontinent in the Soviet policy. 'In the last analysis', he wrote, 'the future will be determined by the cold fact that Russia, China, and India represent a crushing majority of people of the world'. 'The shortest route to Paris', he added, 'runs through Calcutta and Peking.'[11] This formulation was in line with the argument that the end of colonialism in Asia and Africa would create socio-economic chaos in capitalist-imperialist countries, and thus would accelerate the working-class movement in the industrialised societies of Western Europe. For the obvious reasons of revolutionary consolidation in Russia and the inadequacy of economic and military resources necessary to support national liberation movements then, the Soviet leaders did not play a significant role in the independence of European colonies in the Indian Ocean region. The preoccupation with European security issues was another reason for less attention to the colonial areas.

In the post-Second World War period, when a great number of colonies attained sovereign status, Soviet relations with newly independent countries were virtually non-existent. There were many reasons for the Soviet Union's relative political isolation from the post-colonial regimes. First, the colonial domination of European powers in Asia that were hostile to the Russians had effectively blocked the Soviet ideological and political influence. Secondly, the Soviet Union could not undertake substantial commitments of economic and military assistance to the post-colonial third world which perhaps influenced the policies of these countries towards the industrial West.

Thirdly, the dogmatism of the Stalinist period that branded the nationalist leaders of post-colonial regimes as no more than 'lackeys' of international imperialism was, in large part, responsible for a low-key third world policy.

The first theoretical formulation of the Soviet third world policy was given by Khruschev at the Twentieth Party Congress in 1956 when he declared that the Asian States 'had proclaimed non-participation in blocs as a principle of their foreign policy' as a vast 'zone of peace' alongside the socialist countries.[12] The 'zone of peace' thesis signified an alliance of interests between the socialist bloc and the non-aligned countries. The role of the leading non-aligned countries, such as Egypt, India and Indonesia, was conceived as fundamental to world peace and stability. Khruschev took important initiatives that were guided by this theorisation to expand economic, military and political relations with the non-socialist but neutral countries. In a pragmatic sense the Soviet overtures towards these countries were largely motivated by a need to cut through the American containment policy on the Soviet periphery. This also indicated the Soviet desire to compete for influence with the Western powers in all important regions of the world. Although the Soviet economic and military resources were insufficient in the 1950s to meet development needs and security in the third world, the modest aid programme she initiated in selective countries and the stance she took on international issues did promote her image as a friend of the peoples of the third world. The Soviet diplomatic and political moves in the third world were aimed at neutralising the Western attempts to depict the USSR as an aggressive and expansionist power. The dogmatism of the Stalin era was replaced by a diplomatic pragmatism which was largely concerned to thwart Western attempts to isolate the USSR. Co-operation with third world nations that had different social systems gained added significance in the context of East-West Cold War.

During the Khruschev era, the Soviet ideologues persistently stressed vital links between the socialist system and the national liberation movements. In a sense, both complemented each other as far as their role in the international system was concerned. From the Soviet point of view the existence of a socialist bloc not only helped the national liberation of colonial societies but it could also substitute for the absence of a working class in the internal transformation of these societies.

After the political demise of Khruschev in 1964, a neo-orthodox, less optimistic and cautious approach to the third world was adopted. A reappraisal of diplomatic gains from an assertive third world diplomacy indicated very few gains. On the doctrinal level, distinction was made between the progressiveness of national democratic elites and scientific socialism. Therefore, Brezhnev and his colleagues reverted to the working class and Marxist-Leninist line, the doctrine held as indispensable and authentic vis-a-vis several other variants of socialism.

A new approach to global competition with the U.S. and the West in the third world was reflected in the Soviet overtures to even 'reactionary' regimes. This change was affected by the desire to broaden the scope of the Soviet diplomatic initiatives in order to seek political advantages. The complexion of the regimes was, then, not as important as their strategic, economic and political significance to the Soviet globalism. Therefore, the major factors that have increasingly influenced the Soviet interest in and policy towards individual third world countries have been: (1) a country's actual or potential strategic importance for the Soviet Union; (2) its importance as a potential market for the Soviet manufactured goods or as a source of relatively inexpensive consumer goods; and (3) the opportunities of competing effectively with either the United States or China in different regions.[13] In view of the realities of competition with the West, the Soviet leaders have played their third world diplomacy skilfully, aiming at advancing the Soviet national interest without compromising the requirement of revolutionary theory.

The Soviet attempts to play a greater and more effective role in the third world gained strength with : (1) the initiation of a military expansion and modernisation programme that was largely influenced by the debacle of the Cuban missile crisis; (2) allocation of significant economic and technological resources for the creation of a world ocean navy and long-range air transport and air reconnaissance capabilities; and (3) the development and expansion of strategic nuclear forces, which not only offset the U.S. strategic superiority but also proved conducive to defining and expanding Soviet national interests in terms of global power. The Soviet Union has gradually succeeded in attaining a global power status and considerable influence in the third world that the West has recognised and learned to live with.

Brezhnev gave a new dimension to the Soviet global role, particularly in defence of the socialist regimes. This is what is generally referred to as the Brezhnev Doctrine. The redefinition of the role of the Soviet armed forces was not restricted merely to the defence of USSR but also to defend other members of the socialist commonwealth. It explains, in large part, the Soviet military capabilities and willingness to use power to prevent indigenous or external attempts directed towards sabotaging the socialist reconstruction. The Soviet intervention in Czechoslovakia (1968) and Afghanistan (1979) are cases in point.

Finally, internal factors such as rapid changes of leadership in the past few years, the alienation of the working class, stagnating industrial production and technological lags, all indirectly constrain the Soviet diplomacy in the third world which has increasingly required a large commitment of military, economic and technological resources.

The post-Second World War international power arrangements gradually accepted the Soviet parity with Western powers, which reinforced the Soviet quest for political influence. The Asian landmass, due to its geographic proximity, anti-Western feelings and unstable conditions, provided substantial advantages to the Soviet leadership in diplomatic manoeuvring. Apart from any drive for warm-water ports, the primary Soviet objective since the Second World War has been the elimination or, the neutralisation of the pervasive Western presence in the Indian Ocean area.[14]

It was Khruschev who decided to make the Soviet fleet a formidable naval power capable of a global role. As the concept of nuclear deterrence gained ground in the Soviet defence strategy, nuclearisation of the Soviet Navy began to receive serious attention. The desire to acquire nuclear parity with the United States led to an over-emphasis on a nuclear navy, which ignored the development of conventional naval power projection capabilities. The U.S. supremacy in nuclear weapons in general and sea-based strategic deterrence in particular influenced Khruschev's security perceptions. Thus, the Soviet Union embarked upon the construction of nuclear-powered, missile-carrying submarines. This was accompanied by a crash programme to develop a hunter-killer submarine system designed to locate, track and destroy enemy submarines.[15]

In the context of doctrinal and technological changes, the Soviet navy has acquired flexibility and tremendous power in the last two decades. In recognition of a major peacetime foreign policy role for the navy, the Soviet leadership has projected its sea power in all important oceans of the world, including the Indian Ocean. The counter-presence of Soviet naval forces has significantly altered the American naval options in a multi-ocean strategic structure.

Political Objectives

The Soviet naval policy in the Indian Ocean reflects a combination of political, economic and strategic interests. In addition to national security considerations, the Soviet naval units also serve certain political objectives. In showing the flag the Soviet navy has been boosting the morale of its clients and arousing the anxiety of pro-Western states.[16] The Soviet presence is also designed, strategically and tractically, to outflank the Chinese. The politics of competitive interests in the Middle East, Western moves in the 'arc of crisis', instability in the Gulf and the quest for strategic parity have all determined the Soviet calculations of her interests in the Indian Ocean region.

A policy link has gradually developed between the Soviet maritime power and her political, economic ideological and military goals in the Indian Ocean. The Soviet naval presence in the Indian Ocean offers her a variety of options in the region: to maintain patron-client relationship, reduce Western influence, counter Chinese initiatives and create strong naval capabilities to meet global strategic needs.[17]

In the political context, the Soviet naval strategy is directed almost entirely towards the Indian Ocean littoral states. The Soviet politico-diplomatic overtures in the region are, however, a post-Stalin phenomenon. The ideological dimensions of Stalinist foreign policy did not give way to realpolitik. In the post-Second World War period, the newly-independent countries of Asia were viewed as mere appendages of the 'metropolises' and their nationalist leaders were branded as 'lackeys of imperialists'. The importance of nationalism was recognised in the liberation movements, but ideologically it was seen as irreconcilable with Marxism-Leninism. Therefore, the post-independence orientation of the new states was considered to be one of 'neo-colonialism'. This ideological foreign policy outlook was hardly conducive to the cultivation of political relations with the new Afro-Asian states.

In the post-Stalinist period, the Soviet policies underwent radical transformation. The bipolar character of international system, Cold War rivalries, the Western threat perceptions and an element of pragmatism added new significance to the Soviet policy towards the Afro-Asian states. The Soviets attempted to counter the Western containment policy by initiating political and diplomatic offensives in the Indian Ocean littorals. In this regard, the Soviet support for non-alignment became a central theme of her Afro-Asian policy. The American rejection of the Non-Aligned Movement as 'hypocrisy' further added to its importance in the Soviet diplomatic endeavours.

India, Indonesia and Egypt acquired a Central position in the Soviet political thrust. Khruschev's 1955 visit to India, Burma and Afghanistan marked the beginning of a new era of the Soviet political influence in the area. The Soviet Union's anti-colonial stance in Africa and her support for national liberation movements also made her an important factor in regional politics.

The intensification of the Sino-Soviet conflict further sharpened the Soviet perception of the relevance of the Indian Ocean region. In this context, India, centrally located and politically one of the most important countries of the Indian Ocean, became the focus of Soviet policies in the area. The Soviets had a unique opportunity to mediate in a major Indo-Pakistani conflict in 1965. Although the role fell to the USSR mainly by Western default, and the Tashkent Conference (1966) did not resolve the disputes, it earned the Soviet Union a great politico-diplomatic success.[18]

After several setbacks in the Arab world, the Soviets achieved remarkable success with India. They became the major suppliers of military equipment to the Indian military forces since 1965. The Indo-Soviet Treaty of 1971 marked the culmination of that process. The Treaty was described as motivated by 'profound interest in Asian and world security' which assumed great importance in the light of situations developing to the south of the Soviet Union. In fact, the Treaty provided the seal of approval for Indian intervention in East Pakistan.

India emerged as central to the Soviet strategy to balance China and play a leading security role in Asia. Extensive efforts were made to counter Paking in regional politics. In the Soviet policy of encircling China, Vietnam and India came to play an important political and strategic role. India has since long considered herself as a potential alternative to China in Asian politics. Her 1974 'peaceful nuclear explosion' and massive armament programme point in this direction. India's emergence as a regional power is compatible with the Soviet politics in Asia.

Over the last three decades the Soviet Union has gained considerable political successes in the Indian Ocean region. India, with her growing military strength, has emerged as a dependable ally in South Asia. In the Middle East, military cooperation with Libya and a treaty of friendship (1980) with Syria equally indicate diplomatic gains and influence. The Soviet involvement in Ethiopia, Mozambique, Iraq and South Yemen also point in the same direction.

Economic Interests

Economic interests are central to the superpowers' presence in the Indian Ocean, regardless of the fact that most interest is focussed on the military and strategic aspects of their presence. The Soviet Union has important non-military maritime interests in the region. With continued expansion of her merchant fleet, the volume of Soviet commercial shipping has significantly increased over the past decades. The Soviets operate one of the largest merchant marine fleets in the world. An important aspect of the large Soviet merchant marine is its ability to conduct trade with the West, and supply economic and military assistance to third world nations in its own ships. Thus, the merchant fleet has become valuable in promoting Soviet economic and political objectives. The rapid expansion of the Soviet merchant marine has been commensurate with her expanded trade and her position as a superpower. In view of accelerated trade and economic programme in Asia and Africa, the Indian Ocean has become an important and legitimate maritime route for the Soviet merchant marine.

During the 1970s, the Indian Ocean region assumed a prominent position in the Soviet economic calculations. In the aftermath of the Bangladesh crisis of 1971, the Soviet Union's relations with South Asia underwent a qualitative change, particularly in the area of trade and arms transfers to India. Brezhnev's 1973 visit to India resulted in a 15-year economic agreement, providing Soviet assistance for India in steel, coalmining, oil exploitation and power generation. In the economic field, the technical know-how and concessional loans provided by the Soviet Union were of immense value to the development of India's heavy industry in strategic sectors. The giant steel, heavy electric and aluminium plants, in addition to 70 other large-scale projects set up with Soviet assistance, accounted for 20 per cent of power generation, 30 per cent of steel production, 60 per cent of heavy electrical machinery, 70 per cent of oil extraction and 30 per cent of metallurgy equipment in India.

The Indian Ocean is also vital to the Soviet communications network. Safeguarding her important shipping route across the Indian Ocean is a strategic requirement for the Soviet Union. The Indian Ocean provides an all-weather link between the Far Eastern provinces of the USSR and Black Sea. The growing usefulness of this route lies in the fact that it has supplemented the trans-Siberian railroad which has been overloaded due to increased inland commerce. In addition, the eastern part of the railway, and particularly the Soviet Pacific Fleet base at Vladivostok, could be vulnerable to a Chinese attack. In the event of a Sino-Soviet conflict, the Indian Ocean would offer an important transportation option to the Soviet Union.

Apart from the Soviet desire for global parity, the Indian Ocean has acquired strategic importance for the Soviets on account of submarine-launched offensive systems. With the increasing use of missile and nuclear warheads, the Indian Ocean has come to be regarded as a 'vast launching pad for missile-firing submarines'.[19] As the southern flank, the Indian Ocean forms the soft underbelly of the Soviets, and thus is central to Soviet strategic considerations. The U.S. deployment of Polaris A-3 nuclear submarines in the early 1960s, though on a temporary basis, the establishment of communication stations in North-West Australia and Ethiopia designed to service nuclear submarines, the creation of BIOT and the development of the Diego Garcia facility could not be viewed as peaceful ventures by the Soviet leadership. From a strategic point, the Arabian Sea and the Persian Gulf have been considered by the Soviet Union as areas for the potential deployment of U.S. sea power. The U.S. lead in 'floating underwater nuclear bases' has made every ocean a deployment area and a potent seaborne strategic threat to the Soviet security. The Soviet initiatives in anti-submarine warfare have lagged far behind the challenge posed by the U.S. submarine-based strategic offensive.

The relatively rapid expansion of the Soviet naval forces in the Indian Ocean might be seen as strategically defensive. The Soviet navy has maintained a constant anti-submarine warfare (ASW) capability in the region. The adequacy and effectiveness of the Soviet ASW capability in the Indian Ocean, however, has been controversial with regard to countering a ballistic missile submarine threat. The Soviet leaders believe that the United States and her NATO allies have focussed on the world oceans in an attempt to gain strategic superiority. The possibility of a three-ocean-based U.S. missile system with a second-strike capability was perceived as a great danger to the Soviet security interests. Therefore, the Soviet quest for deterrence in the Indian Ocean necessitated a credible naval presence to counter the American threat to her political and security interests in the area. It may be assumed that even the absence of U.S. nuclear submarines would not exclude the Northern Indian Ocean from the strategic calculations of the Soviet Union due to its geo-physical significance.

The Soviet naval deployment in the Indian Ocean should also be seen in the strategic context of the Sino-Soviet disputes. The Soviet containment policy against China is aimed at sea-denial tactics as also to isolate the Chinese as a factor in Asian politics.[20] At present, China lacks a blue-water capability and therefore does not present a significant naval challenge in the Indian Ocean. In an operational sense, the Soviet naval presence, which aims at countering American influence, would also serve to balance the Chinese entry into the Indian Ocean.

The Soviet intervention in Afghanistan was considered 'part of an effort to win warm-water ports coveted since the days of Peter the Great'.[21] In purely military terms, a Soviet overland drive to sea could have been accomplished by crossing the deserts of Baluchistan.[22] But the Soviet Union avoided further extension of her presence due to consolidation problems in Afghanistan.

In the context of Indian Ocean developments, the Soviets have substantially built up the major Vietnam military base of Cam Ranh Bay for use by their naval and air forces in South-east Asia. Situated on the south-east coast of Vietnam, Cam Ranh Bay has become Moscow's most important supply base for Pacific Fleet warship halfway between Vladivostok and the Indian Ocean. The natural anchorage at Cam Ranh Bay and the extension of the port installations can accommodate even the biggest Soviet warships. The Soviet Union has also built piers and other facilities to service nuclear submarines at Cam Ranh Bay. However, the Soviet naval facilities are neither substantial nor comparable to those of America. Moscow has apparently preferred to keep its presence in the Indian Ocean minimal following the loss of Berbera.

The Western debate over the Soviet politico-strategic objectives in the Indian Ocean has not brought forth any concrete set of verifiable propositions. The interpretations of the Soviet moves vary from legitimate security and economic interests to serious threats of expansion and domination of the Persian Gulf region. The Soviet naval deployments and capabilities in the Indian Ocean represent a combination of flag-showing force and area familiarisation detachments oriented to an anti-Polaris and anti-carrier role with the additional objective of political gains. Another factor affecting the Soviet naval presence is China with whom she competes for political influence and strategic advantage in Asia. It is logical to assume that the Soviet Union has important communication and economic interests in the region which make her equally dependent on assured freedom of the sea lanes. The future of the Soviet presence would seem to depend also on the developments in submarine missile technology. Missiles already in service in the Soviet navy make it possible to keep enemy targets under threat without leaving home waters. Without regard to new options to counter SLBMs, however, the Indian Ocean will continue to be an area of strategic and political interest to the Soviet Union. The Soviet navy would post a serious threat to any Western attempt to take over Middle Eastern oil fields or to maintain a status quo in the Persian Gulf through military intervention in the wake of internal instability.

Analysis and Evaluation of the U.S. Strategy

The Indian Ocean region has witnessed a rapid transformation of its political and strategic environment in the past few decades. The fall of the monarchy in Iran, the Soviet intervention in Afghanistan, the Persian Gulf war and the deep rooted political problems in Turkey clearly suggest new patterns of instability in the area. This zone of crises has undermined the U.S. and the Western position and has created new opportunities for the Super Powers. According to some analysts, the diminishing U.S. influence and power in the Indian Ocean region is the result of three decades of 'strategic neglect'.[23] The region did not figure prominently in the post-war global strategy of the United States. The North Atlantic region and the Pacific basin remained the main foci of American power and strategic infrastructure. With the exception of a token U.S. 'Middle East Fleet' of three antiquated naval vessels, the security of the Indian Ocean/Persian Gulf depended heavily on the residual elements of Great Britain's imperial power. Despite serious gaps in the capability of the British forces and early signs of British retreat from the area, the U.S. abstained from establishing a credible presence. Even a prompt British withdrawal of forces from east of Suez in 1968 did not change the American perception of the Indian Ocean as a low priority area.

However, the Soviet naval deployments following the British decision on a total withdrawal from the region, the Soviet and Cuban involvement in Africa and the repercussions of the Arab-Israeli conflict of 1973 and the ensuring oil embargo significantly altered the threat perception in the American defence community. It prompted and intensified efforts in the United States regarding future security policies in the area and the establishment of a credible deterrent posture.

America's 'strategic neglect' of the Indian Ocean/Persian Gulf region can be explained by three widely -held assumptions within the U.S. policy community: the non-existence of any meaningful relationship between visible U.S. military power and regional political stability, the legitimacy of a Soviet naval build-up in view of its 'confrontation' with China, and the lack of a serious threat to the Western economic interests.[24] All of these assumptions have proved to have had catastrophic long-term consequences for the American strategy in the Indian Ocean. 'Strategic neglect' explains only one variable, namely, default by the American policy-makers. The changing political environment of the region and the intensity of the crises are too complex to be explained by a single-variable approach. The Soviet conventional military superiority in some adjacent regions, as well as zealous anti-West indigenous and regional forces, it was feared, might render American military projection ineffective.

The pro-West forces in the region were shaken by the militancy of Iran and Soviet occupation of Afghanistan. These 'twin crises' increased their sense of vulnerability. The U.S. response, the Carter Doctrine,[25] took the form of a more visible military presence aimed at restoring confidence in the American power and determination to guarantee regional security. Ironically, despite open declarations of keeping the Super Powers out of the region, many regimes depend on the U.S. for their ultimate security against the perceived Soviet and regional threats.

The current U.S. naval deployment in the Indian Ocean is preponderant and superior to the Soviet base facilities and naval capabilities. An essential element of the U.S. Indian Ocean strategy is the expanded base facility at Diego Garcia.

Without such a base, the U.S. Navy would find it logistically very taxing to support naval operations in the area. Diego Garcia has become the only stable U.S. facility in the Indian Ocean because it is away from the restricted waters and narrow straits and has the capacity to receive supplies directly from the American metropolitan base.

REFERENCES

1. *Survival* (London), 22 (July/August 1980). See a statement by Harold Brown, p. 71.
2. T.B. Millar, 'Geopolitics and Military/Strategic Potential', in Alvin J. Cottrell and R.M. Burell (eds.), *The Indian Ocean: Its Political, Economic, and Military Importance,* p. 67.
3. Monoranjan Bezbourah, *U.S. Strategy in the Indian Ocean: The International Response* (New York : Praeger, 1977), p. 141.
4. U.S. Congress, House Committee on Foreign Affairs, Subcommittee International Operations, Fiscal Year 1983 Supplemental Authorization Request for the Department of State and U.S. Information Agency, 97th Congress, 2nd Session (Washington, D.C. : GPO, 1983), Statement of Nicholas A. Veliotes, p. 8.
5. Andrew J. Pierre (ed.), *Arms Transfers and American Foreign Policy* (New York : New York University Press, 1979), p. 1.
6. U.S. Arms Control and Disarmament Agency, *World Military Expenditures and Arms Transfers, 1972-1982* (Washington, D.C.: ACDA , April 1984), pp. 95-8.
7. Merrill Sheils and Jerry Buckley, 'The Mineral Crisis', *News Week,* 10 November, 1980, p. 98.
8. U.S. Department of Defense, Joint Chiefs of Staff, United States Military Posture for FY 1978, by General George Brown, USAF, 1977, p. 102.
9. Monoranjan Bezboruah, *U.S. Strategy in the Indian Ocean,* p. 39.
10. *Washington Post,* 24 February 1982, p. A20.
11. U.S. Congress, House Committee on Foreign Affairs, *The Indian Ocean : Political and Strategic Future,* 92nd Congress, 1st Session (Washington, D.C.: GPO, 1973), testimony of Chester Bowles, p. 53.
12. *Pravda,* 15 February 1956, p. 2.
13. Roger E. Kanet, 'The Soviet Union and the Developing Countries: Policy or Policies', in *Soviet Economic and Political Relations with the Developing World* (New York : Praeger, 1975), p. 12.

14. Hermann F. Elits, 'Security Considerations in the Persian Gulf', *International Security*, 5 (Fall 1980), p. 81.
15. Oles M. Smolansky, 'Soviet Entry into the Indian Ocean: An Analysis', in Alvin J. Cottrell and R.M. Burrell (eds.), *The Indian Ocean : its Political, Economic, and Military Importance,* p. 340.
16. Elmo R. Zumwalt, Jr., 'Gorshkov and his Navy, *Orbis*, 24 (Fall 1980), p. 505.
17. J. Bowyer Bell, 'Strategic Implications of the Soviet Presence in Somalia', *Orbis* 19 (Summer 1975), pp. 408-10.
18. Golam W. Choudhury, *Brezhnev's Collective Security Plan for Asia* (North Carolina Central University : Center for Strategic and International Studies, 1976), pp. 1-2.
19. Hanson W. Baldwin, 'The Indian Ocean Context, Part I : The Soviet Union's Increasing Interest', *New York Times,* 20 March 1972, p. 37.
20. William F. Kickman, 'Soviet Naval Policy in the Indian Ocean', *U.S. Naval Institute Proceedings*, 105 (August, 1979), p. 44.
21. Elmo R. Zumwaltin Jr., *'Gorshkov and his Navy'*, p. 506.
22. Edward N. Luttwak in Commentary, April, 1980; Ernst Van Der Beugel, 'After Afghanistan', *Survival,* 22 (November/December 1980), pp. 246-7.
23. Thomas H. Moorer and Alvin J. Cottrell, 'The Search for U.S. Bases in the Indian Ocean: a Last Chance', *Strategic Review,* 8 (Spring 1980), pp. 30-31.
24. *Ibid.*
25. President Carter outlined his doctrine in his State of the Union address to Congress (January 1980). The doctrine relates to U.S. readiness to use military force if necessary to protect its vital interests in the Gulf. *The Times,* 25 January, 1980.

CHAPTER IV

India and the Indian Ocean Politics

Political Interests of India in the Indian Ocean

India is one of the major regional powers in the Indian Ocean area. She has vital political and foreign policy interests in the region. Most of the fortyseven Indian Ocean littoral and hinterland countries are "non-aligned". India can play a leading role through the unity and the movement of the non-aligned countries for the implemention of 1971 U.N. resolution of giving Indian Ocean a status of 'Peace Zone', free from big power rivalry, foreign military bases and nuclear arms. Any effort to distort or dilute this 'Peace Zone' concept of the Indian Ocean by any power would not be acceptable to India. Industrially developing and culturally closer to many Indian Ocean countries, India can play a vital role in making the Indian Ocean region an area of 'high solidarity'. The most important challenge for India's diplomacy is to improve her own image among the Indian Ocean countries which have a number of misgivings regarding India's nuclear status, military strength, industrial and technological potential and its friendship with the Soviet Union . Some of these misgivings have risen from the propaganda of some countries having vested interests in the region. At the political level, India has to realise that the Indian Ocean region is the key to her national security and economic progress and that she can ill-afford even the smallest degree of indifference towards this region.

The important planks on which India's Indian Ocean policy is based are :

(i) The opposition to the big-power military presence in the region - a 'peace zone' strategy;

(ii) The improvement of her own image by removing misgiving about her Indian Ocean policy;

(iii) The promotion of regional consciousness, cooperation and community feeling among the Indian Ocean countries and formation of an Indian Ocean community.

Liquidation of colonialism has been of the main political planks of India's foreign policy and is equally applicable to the Indian Ocean region. Opposition to colonialism and support to the cause of freedom movements in the region are the most important aspects of India's foreign policy. After independence, India embarked on the programme of bringing solidarity among Afro-Asian countries to oppose colonialism and explotation through Asian and non-aligned conferences. Her policies were particularly oriented towards the Afro-Asian region. As early as 1951, Pandit Jawaharlal Nehru, the first Prime Minister of India, enunciated the doctrine of the 'Peace Area' in Afro-Asian region which should be free from cold war rivalry and military alignments.

The Indian Ocean started engaging India's attention after the arrival of the U.S. Task Force from its Pacific-based Seventh Fleet in 1963. But at that time, in spite of the hue and cry by the opposition members in the Parliament, the Government did not take a serious view of the problem and did not lodge an official protest. Pandit Jawaharlal Nehru, justified the same on the ground of 'freedom of seas' and did not consider it a grave threat to India's security. This attitude might have perhaps been due to the benevolent attitude of the U.S. at the time of the Chinese aggression in 1962. Some analysts are of the opinion that in the early sixties India lacked the political will to oppose the naval presence of the U.S. and her other allies.

The Soviet Union brought to the notice of Lal Bahadur Shastri, the then Prime Minister of India, the presence of 'polaris submarines' of the United States in the Indian Ocean when he visited that country in 1965. The Indo-Soviet concern was also shown in their joint communique issued on the occasion.

In 1967, India's position regarding Indian Ocean was, however, more clear when Foreign Minister, M.C. Chagla, during the calling attention motion in Lok Sabha condemned the very idea of detaching some islands from Mauritius and Seychelles before granting them freedom by U.K. and called it against the U.N. resolutions. He also opposed the establishment of military bases in the Indian Ocean which might increase tension in the region. He assured to represent against such bases to the government concerned and also to take up the matter in the United Nations.[1] But it seems that at that time India was convinced that Diego-Gracia base was to be used by the U.K. and the U.S.A. as a communication centre to have 'transit staging and refuelling facilities' in the region for their naval vessels, as these two countries assured that they had no idea of setting up a military base in the region.[2] On June 22, 1967, M.C. Chagla informed the Lok Sabha about this assurance, but the opposition members termed the government stand as 'callous' and warned the Government about the possibility of creation of a military base at Diego-Garcia and its impact on the security of India.[3]

But very soon India's policy towards the Indian Ocean became more realistic. India welcomed the British decision to withdraw its trops from the east of Suez. Mrs. Indira Gandhi, the then Indian Prime Minister, outrightly rejected the theory of so-called 'power vacuum' advanced by some countries and called it a trick of big powers to justify their presence in the region. These powers were, however, compelled to leave the region due to the growing feelings of nationalism in the region and due to their own politico-economic compulsions.[4] During the tour of some South-East Asian countries in May, 1969, Mrs. Gandhi reiterated that if any vacuum was created it ought to be filled by the local powers themselves and not by outside powers. She said, "There can be no question of vacuum if we make our economics viable and our societies stable".[5] India's External Affairs Minister, Mr. Dinesh Singh, quoting the Prime Minister, informed Lok Sabha that "going away of the British navy has not created vacuum... We welcome their withdrawal. It was a symbol of domination in Asia. I am surprised and in many ways humiliated when my countrymen say what will happen if the British go away. We have got to prepare ourselves to meet the challenges that come and it can be done with a measure of self-respect, dignity and self-reliance and not looking to Washington or Moscow".[6]

The Western propaganda of 'power vacuum' might not have made any impact on India but it did work favourably in some countries of the region. The British decision of withdrawal from the Indian Ocean was received with alarm by the Governments of Iran, Kuwait, Saudi Arabia, Bahrain, Abu Dhabi, Singapore, Malaysia, Newzealand and Austrialia.

The Soviet Union too did not miss the opportunity and started sending its task forces in the region since 1968. With its arrival on the scene, Indian apprehension came true that the presence of one Super Power will invariably attract the other Super Power. The Russian entry into the Ocean was exaggerated by the Western military strategists to strengthen their own position and to prepare a favourable psychological climate in the region to accommodate the United States and its collaborators. The coming up of U.S. - U.K. military base at Diego- Garcia and the arrival of the task forces of the two Super Powers in the Indian Ocean made India aware of the stark realities of big power rivalry for gaining influence and hold on the region. She started strongly opposing the alien presence in the Ocean, which was considered a big threat to its national security and peace in the region. India focussed her attention at the political level by propagating the concept that the Indian Ocean instead of being a 'high conflict area' should be a 'zone of peace and cooperation', free from big-power rivalry and competition. Hereafter, the Indian Government took up this issue at various levels and in various fora within the country and abroad.

In the country the issue was debated in both the Houses of Parliament, the press and in various academic seminars and conferences. References to the Indian Ocean problem were made by Indian leaders in their statements and even in the joint communiques issued after the visit of foreign dignitaries. At the international level, fora like U.N. Commonwealth and Non-aligned Conference were used to express the Indian view point regarding this problem.[7]

Swaran Singh, the then Indian Minister for External Affairs, expressed his Government's opposition to the foreign presence in the Indian Ocean in terms of their warships and bases. He also reiterated India's firm commitment to the Lusaka declaration of non-aligned countries in September 1970 which had called upon the big powers to keep their hands off from the Indian Ocean.[8] Jagjivan Ram, the then Defence Mini- ster, told the Lok Sabha on December 14, 1970, and Rajya Sabha on June 9, 1971 regarding Indian opposition to the presence of foreign warships in the Indian Ocean. He emphasized that it was likely to create tension in the region. The Parliament also showed concern over the deployment of the Task Force of the U.S. 7th fleet in the Bay of Bengal at the time of the Indo-Pak War 1971. India's External Affairs Minister, Swaran Singh, on November 30, 1972 explained India's Indian Ocean policy in Rajya Sabha in these words : "India's policy is to keep the Indian Ocean free from nuclear weapons." He also referred to India's effort to create consensus against the presence of big powers through United Nations and Non-aligned Conference.[9]

During the Foreign Affairs debate in the Parliament, Deputy Minister for External Affairs, Surendra Pal Singh, informed the Lok Sabha regarding the presence of foreign ships in the Indian Ocean, both conventional and nuclear, and called this development as a potential danger and expressed the government's anxiety and concern over it.[10]

The entry of the U.S. nuclear power aircraft carrier Kitty Hawk in the Indian Ocean was also resented in the Lok Sabha in March 1974. Swaran Singh told the House that the Government of India would mobilise world opinion against the American bases in the Indian Ocean. He expresed opposition "to the presence of any foreign naval force or the establishment of any bases in this region."[11] He further clarified that India provided only normal bunkering facilities to the ships of friendly countries such as the USA, UK, France and the USSR. He also mentioned the necessity of a dialogue and discussion among the littoral countries and the other maritime powers whose presence was there is the Indian Ocean to adopt some restraint in this direction.

The Janata Government also expressed concern regarding the presence of big powers' naval force in the Indian Ocean and over the suspension of US-Soviet negotiations over arms limitations in the Ocean. "The presence of Great Powers in the Indian Ocean is a cause of tension and insecurity" was the Government's considered view.[12] The Janata Government also showed firm faith in the implemention of Peace Zone concept through more cooperation in the UN by big powers. It wanted to create a favourable opinion for Peace Zone among the littoral countries of the Indian Ocean through bilateral diplomacy.

While the earlier government did not accept the presence of Soviet bases in the Indian Ocean region, the government of Mrs. Indira Gandhi held that the Western powers' involvement in the Indian Ocean region was responsible for the Soviet intervention in Afghanistan in 1979.[13] W. Averell Harriman, a prominent member of the U.S. Committee on Foreign Relations, also expressed his fears that the American presence in the Indian Ocean would definitely attract the Soviet Union there.[14] The U.S. opposition to the very concept of Peace Zone resolution in the Indian Ocean, which got mandate from the majority of the Indian Ocean countries in the United Nations in 1971, was act or subversion from the Indian point of view.[15] On the other hand, the USSR, which also voted against the resolution in 1971, expressed its willingness to work for Peace Zone concept on the basis of equality with other big powers.[16]

In the non-aligned forum, India supported all those resolutions which opposed the big power presence in the Indian Ocean. As early as 1964, in the Cairo Non-Aligned Summit Conference the member countries viewed with concern the entry of the U.S. task force in the Indian Ocean and called it a "calculated attempt to intimidate the emerging countries of Africa and Asia and an unwarranted extension of neo-colonialism and imperialism".[17]

At the Lusaka Non-Aligned Conference in 1970, a consenus among the member countries was created in favour of the Indian Ocean as a zone of peace; free from big power rivalry, their military bases and nuclear weapons. Speaking on the occasion, Mrs. Indira Gandhi said : "We would like the Indian Ocean to be an area of peace and cooperation; military bases of outside powers would create tensions and great power rivalry".[18] Later, addressing the 90-nation Non-Aligned Foreign Ministers Conference (February 9-13, 1981), she underlined the two major tasks before the movement, namely, restitution of detente, and reduction of the big power military presence in the Indian Ocean.

In the Singapore Conference of the Commonwealth Countries in January 1971, India supported Sri Lanka's memorandum expressing concern over the growing militarization of the Indian Ocean. The then External Affairs Minister of India, Swaran Singh, condemned the step by step transformation of the Indian Ocean into an area of big power rivalry and tension much to the detriment of the interests of littoral states.

In the United Nations, India played a key role in mobilising public opinion in favour of Peace Zone. India was co-sponsor of the resolution moved by Sri Lanka regarding Peace Zone in the Indian Ocean and gave unqualified support to this concept during the debate in the United Nations. It culminated in the declaration of the Indian Ocean as a Zone of Peace vide its resolution 2832 (xxvi) on December 16, 1971.[19] To impart further momentum to the resolution on Peace Zone, India and Sri Lanka jointly sponsored the same resolution for the consideration of U.N. Main Political Committee in 1972. India was also the member of the 15-member Ad Hoc Committee to further study the 'Peace Zone' proposal for implementation. K. Subrahmanyam, the Director of the Institute for Defence Studies and Analyses, was one of the three members asked by the Secretary General of the U.N. to prepare a factual statement regarding the big powers' military presence in the Indian Ocean. Ever since the acceptance of the concept of 'Peace Zone' in the Indian Ocean, the United Nations took up this issue almost every year but nothing worthwhile came out due the total indifference of the great maritime powers. The U.N. decided in 1974 to convene an 'Indian Ocean Conference' which, however, never took place. None of the permanent members of the Security Council such as USA, USSR, France and UK showed willingness to attend the same. Instead, their naval presence in the Indian Ocean increased day by day showing utter disregard to the popular U.N. resolution regarding 'Peace Zone'. The U.N. Ad Hoc Committee, which was later enlarged to 46 members, faced difficulty in functioning as a preparatory committee for the Conference due to the differences among the non-aligned and East European countries on the one hand and the Western countries on the other. The latter insisted for harmonization of views and the improvement of political and security climate in the area as a precondition.[20] The former did not insist on the same and believed that the convening the Indian Ocean Conference itself would be a stage in the harmonization process within the Indian Ocean region.[21]

Peace Zone Strategy : A Critical Evaluation

The cardinal point of India's Ocean policy rests upon the 'Peace Zone' concept which opposes the military presence of extra-regional powers in any form in the Indian Ocean and tries to forge more meaningful ties within the region. Though this concept has not succeeded much, it seems that there is no better alternative. The increasing number of super and big powers' armada in the Indian Ocean, their continuous search for bases in the region, growing intra-regional rivalaries and arms race, non-co-operation of big maritime powers to accept the Peace Zone concept, varying perception of the Indian Ocean countries regarding the presence of the big powers in the region and double standard followed by some of them in this respect forced by their foriegn and domestic compulsions, are the few reasons which could be attributed to its failure. Some scholars started calling it a 'dead horse' and 'utopian concept' which could hardly be implemented.

However, if continued to be handled properly in the non-aligned and other regional fora like ASEAN,OAU and Arab League, it could put the super and big powers in an embarrassing situation and force them to accept a balanced withdrawal from the Ocean. P.K.S. Namboodri does not agree with the view that Peace Zone issue is an unrealistic proposition and a short-sighted approach. He calls it "yet another aspect of mankind's struggle for world peace".[22] India should strive to bring co-operation among littoral countries by keeping 'Peace Zone' campaign alive, so that this crucial diplomatic offensive against the big power presence in the Indian Ocean may not lose its impact. It is desirable that India should not confine her efforts to disarmament and arms control only. She should also give proper weightage to the development strategy of this region. For this purpose the Indian Ocean problem may be made a part of discussions of South-South and North-South dialogue. The then

External Affairs Minister of India, P.V.Narasimaha Rao, while replying to the questions in Lok Sabha in July 1980, denied that India was adopting a lukewarm attitude towards the Indian Ocean. He, however, agreed that the government should be little more strident and aggressive on issues involving the Indian Ocean.[23]

But it is a hard fact that mentioning 'Peace Zone' at various national and international fora and in joint communiques has now become a ritual and is gradually losing its impact. Without the enthusiastic follow-up action on the part of littoral and hinterland states, nothing could be achieved in this respect. For the successful implementation of 'Peace Zone' concept in the region it has been suggested that :

(1) Intra-regional arms race (including nuclear) should be kept under check with the co-operation of the big powers.

(2) Intra-regional conflicts should be resolved through some intra-regional machanism without providing any opportunity of interference by the big powers. Sri Lanka's suggestion regarding the "creation of a Commission for settling boundary disputes and for formulation of code of conduct to ward off, mitigate and resolve controversial questions among the non-aligned countries"[24] in Colombo Non-Aligned Conference (1976) was a proper step in this direction which was supported by India. Unfortunately no follow-up action took place to implement the proposal. For example, non-aligned efforts failed to resolve Iran-Iraq war.

(3) To ventilate the view-points of all the countries of region, a permanent forum be provided to hold Indian Ocean conference regularly with a view to minimise big powers' manipulations behind the scene.

(4) To have understanding among the countries of the Indian Ocean region for not providing any military bases to any outside power.

(5) The countries of the region should learn to be self-reliant rather than dependent on foreign economic aid which has many strings.

(6) The countries of the region should secure co-operation

from super-powers to reduce their presence in the Indian Ocean from low level balanced presence to non-presence.[25]

(7) Littoral states have taken advantage of the inner contradictions of the Communist world as well as of the Western Block. It could be exploited to seek support of some of them for the 'Peace Zone' concept. Economic and political pressure might prove useful against the extra-regional powers and might ultimately help in evolving "Indian Ocean Community".[26]

(8) Having low military capability, the littoral countries can only hope to generate psychological pressure upon the great powers to achieve their goal. For this purpose unity is essential.[27]

India's Indian Ocean Policy is under perpetual strain within India and outside as well. Parliamentary debates in India reveal that Indian parliamentarians are divided into various ideological camps. According to their ideological affinities they perceive the threat from different big powers. For some parliamentarians the U.S. presence is doing more harm, for others Russian presence has aggravated the situation. The Government of India appealed several times that the Parliament should oppose the military presence of all outside powers in any form without any reservation.

Though most of the Indian Ocean littoral countries have voted for the Peace Zone concept in the Indian Ocean in the United Nations, a few of them are following a double standard suited to their domestic needs and self-interests.

As long as the American bases, their military presence in the region and their military aid to their former military allies remain, it is felt that India has to look towards the Soviet Union for her security.[28] This makes India a Russian stooge in the eyes of Western strategic analysts. But in reality, India will neither relish a satellite role under Russian tutelage nor will it welcome its military intervention in any part of the Indian Ocean. It is opposed to the military presence of all foreign powers in the region irrespective of their nationality or ideology. It is in consonance with its foreign policy goals in the region.

Under the circumstances, forging unity among the Indian Ocean littoral countries, whether politically or for security reasons, seems to be an uphill task. India's 'soft corner' for Russia (due to her time-tested friendship), non-reconciliation with Pakistan, its growing military power (including naval) and growing nuclear capability (for peaceful purposes) and its industrial strength are seen with suspicion by the littoral countries and the Western world. Strategists, scholars and diplomats add fuel to fire by giving such views: "Indian Ocean is on the point of becoming an Indian Lake"[29] and "India, heartened by its victory against Pakistan in 1971, will feel encouraged to aspire to be the dominant naval power in the immediate environment".[30]

At the political level, there is a great need to counter this propaganda. But India's economic dependence on foreign countries and her own ideological inhibitions always act as restraining factors in projecting her power like the other big maritime powers.[31] Moreover, India which has won her freedom after a long struggle with a colonial power cannot think in terms of dominating its neighbours. It should be made clear to the countries of the region that India's growing naval strength is only for her own maritime defence and not for achieving pre-eminence in the Indian Ocean region. She opposes the concept of domination of one power over the other and is genuinely interested in the Peace Zone concept in the Indian Ocean. Her moral and political stand during Bangladesh war (1971) needs world-wide publicity so that she is not gravely misunderstood abroad. The big power propaganda against India is an effort on their part to obtain themselves a favourable foothold in the countries of the region by creating fear psychosis against other big littoral countries. Thus the biggest political problem for India in the Indian Ocean region is to project her image in a proper diplomatic perspective and to evolve an active Indian Ocean policy to forge unity among the countries of the region.

Conclusion

India has many challenging political problems in the Indian Ocean region, such as opposing the extra-regional military presence, establishing her political and cultural links with the littoral countries, projecting her own image in a proper way as a regional power and making efforts to convert this region from low to high solidarity area by helping the evolution an Indian Ocean Community. India has been opposing the big power military presence in the Indian Ocean region, through her Parliament, press and at the international fora like the U.N., the Commonwealth and the Non-aligned Movement. She politically rejects the so-called 'vacuum theory' in the Indian Ocean which is being propounded by the U.S. and her allies to justify their military presence after the partial withdrawal of the UK from the region.

Most of the Indian Ocean countries, including India, have supported the proposal of Sri Lanka that Indian Ocean should be declared as a 'Zone of Peace and Co-operation - free from military presence of the extra-regional powers'. But largely economic dependence, and for some countries even security dependence on big powers, has never allowed them to sincerely pursue the cause of Peace Zone. Owing to their vested interest and imaginary fear of the domination of the regional powers, a number of Indian Ocean countries are themselves sabotaging the cause of 'Peace Zone' in the region. Moreover, almost incessant regional wars never allowed this Ocean to be the real 'Zone of Peace'. The big powers had been skillfully exploiting the regional differences to further their politico-military and economic interests by aggravating the situation through proxies.

Some intra-regional organisation is required to settle the intra-regional disputes, since most of the peace-keeping organisations are becoming almost ineffective. The potential of the Non-aligned Forum may be fully explored for resolving these conflicts without the interference of the big powers. The countries of the Indian Ocean region will have to understand that no alien power will give them the guarantee of peace until they realise its importance themselves and endeavour hard in this direction.

India has to adopt a 'development strategy' in the region as an important plank of her 'Peace Zone' strategy. Politically, Indian Ocean should not only be discussed in terms of arms control and disarmament but also in terms of intra-regional economic co-operation. The most important challenge to India is to improve her image among the Indian Ocean countries which harbour a large number of misgivings due to her nuclear status, her stand on nuclear weapon free zone in South Asia, her military strength, her industrial, technological and scientific potential and her peace treaty with the Soviet Union. To project her image in a proper perspective, India has rightly established bilateral economic and cultural links with more than 22 countries of the India Ocean region.

Some experts feel that 'Peace Zone' rhetoric has now become obsolete and some new political strategy should be formed in relation to the Indian Ocean. But for the militarily weak and industrially backward nations of this region there can be no better policy than the present one. This policy needs to be strengthened by forging intra-regional unity through mutual co-operation and evolving an Indian Ocean Community. Any compromise with the presence of the big powers will accelerate the pace of their interventionist policies in the region. It would be better for India to strengthen the South Asian co-operation if larger Indian Ocean Community is not possible due to many regional asymmetries. South Asian co-operation, economic and political, is the key to her peace and prosperity with a large number of countries coming within the orbit.

The Indian Ocean region has great economic significance to India. She depends for more than 60 per cent of her energy needs on the Persian Gulf region. Her necessary supplies of minerals like copper, zinc, lead, nickel, tin and aluminium come from this region. She also depends on this region for her vital needs of food, chemicals and fertilizers. The region accounted for nearly 34 per cent annual imports and 22 per cent annual exports in 1979-80. Her trade with the region has risen to seven times since 1971, and her non-traditional items like engineering goods are becoming popular in the region. The Indian Ocean region provides a key market to the Indian goods and gives India ample opportunities for turn-key jobs and joint enterprises. India has about 160 joint enterprises in the region which are either established or are in the process of being established. A large number of technical experts from India are serving in various countries of the Indian Ocean under technical co-operation programme. The Indian Government will have to be watchful that substandard machines, technology or goods are not transferred to the countries of this region if she wants to improve her economic relations with them. Less capital investment, insufficient industrialisation, relative technological and scientific backwardness in comparison with the Western nations and Japan are the reasons which come in India's way in establishing sound economic links with the countries of this region. The creation of Economic Division under the External Affairs Ministry is a step in the right direction to promote and strengthen politico-economic links in the region.

India's role in North and South dialogue to protect the third world countries' economic interests and exploitation is commendable. In order to obtain a better return for the raw material of the Indian Ocean countries, there is a great need to establish an OPEC type organisation so that their valuable mineral resources should not go at throw away prices. Unity among the countries of the Indian Ocean region would itself work against their economic exploitation. The availability of metallic and non-metallic resources in the continental shelf, and deep sea basin and living resources in the economic zone of India raise her hopes for future prosperity. Impressive oil and natural gas production from her off-shore wells has reduced her dependence on the Gulf region at least by 15 per cent. Sound management of these oceanic resources is essential for her economic well-being.

With her mobilisation of opinion of a large number of member countries, India has successfully protected her own interest and that of the other developing maritime nations in the Third Sea Law Conference sponsored by the United Nation (UNCLOS III). The major gains of this Conference are the extension of territorial sea limit from 3 nautical miles (n.m.) to 12 n.m., recognition of 24 n.m. contiguous zone and 200 n.m. exclusive economic zone alongwith a large continental shelf. On the basis of consensus in UNCLOS III regarding the aforesaid maritime zones, India assumed legal right over such zones in her waters in 1976 through passing the Maritime Zone Act in the Parliament.

This gives India the sovereign control over nearly 2 million sq. km. waters as exclusive economic zone and 1 million sq. km. submerged land as continental shelf and continental margin for the economic exploitation. Oceanographic research has proved that these zones are full of living and non-living resources.

India, alongwith the group of 77 nations, successfully opposea, through UNCLOS III, the exploitation of the deep sea bed resources in the waters beyond national jurisdiction by a few technologically advanced countries. Such resources were considered a 'common heritage' and their management was given to the United Nations for the welfare of entire mankind. India's interest and investment in the deep sea mining capability was recognised by the United Nations which granted her the status of one of the pioneer investers in the field of sea mining. India is the only developing country to gain this status. The perfection of deep sea exploration and exploitation technology will enable her to play a leading role in the Indian Ocean region in that regard.

India has not only to plan for the defence and security of her long coastline, a large number of islands, ports and the territorial waters, but she has also to provide security to her prestigious industries like nuclear, satellite, petro-chemical and shipping, situated mainly on her coastal region. Important coastal towns, ports and harbours need integrated defence against any sea or air-borne attack, sabotage and infiltration.

In the Indian Ocean region there can be two areas of co-operation: economic and security. Though there will be many misconceptions regarding security co-operation yet the military resources, particularly naval, can be mobilised to ensure safety and security for the international shipping and coverflights passing through the waters and air space of the Indian Ocean, its narrow sea straits and littoral territorial waters. This will remove at least one of the pretexts of the big powers to justify their military presence in the region. If India does not want the involvement of big powers in the affairs of her small Indian Ocean neighbours, she should be ready to render them security help from naval point of view whenever there is a need. It is now a major requirement for the Indian navy that it should project itself in the region as a force of peace, co-operation and development unlike that of the big powers, which is mainly used of intervention, intrusion and coercion.

The sea-borne threat to India emanates from the military presence of super and big powers in the Indian Ocean region and from some militarily strong regional powers. The nature of threat from the super and big powers will be more indirect which may come in the form of intervention, proxy wars and nuclear blackmail while threat from the regional powers will be more direct and may lead to naval combat in the Indian waters. The chances of direct confrontation of super powers in the region are remote due to the inherent danger of a catastrophic Third World War. But their indirect support in terms of intelligence and arms transfer at the time of intra-regional wars cannot be ruled out which may shift the balance in favour of their allies in the region.

The significance of the Indian Ocean increased in 1980s as it was considered important in the Space War programme of the two Super Powers. For an effective Space War strategy, an extensive network of ground and space-based command, control communication and intelligence network is necessary. For this, five Ground Based Electro-Optical Deep Space Surveillance (GEODSS) systems would be required by the USA, one of which is going to be installed at Diego Garcia. Such military developments in the Indian Ocean are naturally disturbing to India which has high security stakes in the region. In the interest of her security she has to be fully alert to appreciate the potential of such new ocean and space based military threats and has to devise some counter-measures.

Indian Ocean Politics - A Challenge to India

K.M. Panikkar rightly pointed out, as early as mid-forties, the strategic importance of the Indian Ocean because it is the highway of European nations to India, the Far East and Australia. It has become increasingly important to the political, strategic and economic interests of the super and big powers. It is called the Ocean of the Future while the Atlantic and the Pacific are thought of as oceans of the past.[32] The control over the Indian Ocean gives direct or indirect control of about 47 littoral, continental and off-shore States of the Indian Ocean which constitute one of the most densely populated areas of the world having nearly 1/3rd of the world population. A unique feature of this region is natural wealth amidst misery, hunger and poverty. There are large deposits of oil, uranium, tin, gold and diamonds. Moreover, the countries of this region are the largest producers of rubber, tea, spices and jute. Other important minerals produced in this region are manganese, cobalt, tungsten, coal, iron ore etc. It is estimated that more than 90% of world's known reserve of chrome ore is located in Rhodesia and South Africa. The entire West is dependent on the Indian Ocean area not only for its raw material needs but for its markets as well. The Soviet Union too is dependent on this Ocean, for 80% of the Soviet seaborne trade passes through the Indian Ocean. The Malacca, the Muscat and and Bab-el-Mandel Straits in the Indian Ocean are of crucial importance to international navigation.

The advancement made in the field of science and technology has added new dimensions to the problem and has whetted the appetite of big powers. Advanced shipping techniques adopted by the Japanese and American fishing vessels result in unimaginably large hauls by suction. Even processing and canning is done on the vessels. This has resulted in denial of good fish to the littoral countries having smaller and ill-equipped fishing vessels. It appears that if such practice continues the Indian Ocean might be completely depleted of fish. It would have an extremely adverse effect on the ecology of the Indian Ocean and the economy of the littoral countries.

Sophistication in the field of weaponry has added to the geo-strategic significance of the Indian Ocean. The rise in the importance of the Indian Ocean coincides with the perfection achieved in submarine sinews of war. The Polaris submarines, which have been in operation in this region, can hit the target anywhere inside the Soviet Union from the Indian Ocean. These submarines can remain under water for three months without any external assistance. They can operate even at the depth of 2000 feet which makes their detection difficult. But Polaris is a thing of the past. The Poseidon and Trident are much more deadly. The Trident missiles are reported to have a range of about 4000 miles compared to Poseidon's 2500 miles and Polaris' 2400 miles. The CEP (circular error probable) of the Poseidon is reported to be half as compared to that of Polaris. The CEP of the Trident would be much less. The plans of creating the ULMS (undersea long range missile system), the NRI, a nuclear powered ocean engineering and research vehicle equipped with nuclear power plant, oceanographic equipment and sensors have made the Indian Ocean an arena of the future battles.[33] It is obvious that the Arabian Sea and the Bay of Bengal would provide the most important area for missile operations against Southern and Central Russia and Western China. A closer examination of the interests of the Super Powers and the response of the regional and sub-regional actors would be instructive for understanding India's strategic dilemma.

The U.S. objectives in the Indian Ocean area have been spelt out in the document 'U.S. Foreign Policy Objectives and Overseas Military Installations' prepared by the Congress Research Service in 1979 for the Committee on Foreign Relations of the U.S. Senate. It says: "The U.S. has both a conventional and perhaps a strategic nuclear military interest in the Indian Ocean region. Military objectives for the U.S. conventional forces include the capability to (1) protect U.S. economic interests in the Persian Gulf region (2) employ or threaten force in support of U.S. diplomatic objectives in the Middle East (3) secure the Indian Ocean air and sea routes against harassment or interdiction (4) intervene in support of other objectives in the littoral, and related to all of these (5) balance Soviet forces in the region and attain superiority in a crisis. The U.S. also possesses a potential strategic nuclear military objective of deploying when necessary or convenient, ballistic missile submarines targeted on the USSR".[34]

The U.S. objectives are far more comprehensive than the ones mentioned above. They are clear and long-ranged. As pointed out earlier, continuous supply of raw material, to feed the large military industrial complexes for the production of deadly weapons, from various underdeveloped countries has to be ensured. The U.S. depends on import of 80% to 100% of the material of more than half of 62 industrial commodities listed as strategic by the defence organisation. There are six essential materials used in the jet engine and the U.S. has to import 5 of these materials - 100% of chromium, cobalt and columbium, 75% of nickel and 24% of tungsten.[35] The U.S. meets as much as 85% of its tin requirements from the countries of this region. Australia supplies zinc, tungsten, thorium, manganese, lead and iron ore. It supplies 65% of titanium which is vital for the U.S. space industries, missile construction and supersonic aircraft.

Another reason of the American penetration of the Indian Ocean is its insistence on the principle of freedom of seas. Its presence in the Indian Ocean, according to an American spokesman, "reinforces proposition that the seas belong to everyone".[36] The apologists of neocolonialism argue that the oceans are so great that a cooperative international effort to develop marine resources for the benefits of all humanity seems logical. There is yet another reason. The downfall of the Shah of Iran, the success of the national liberation movements in Yemen, Ethiopia, Mozambiqe and other countries, the presence of Soviet troops in Afghanistan and the disintegration of its politico-military alliances prompted the U.S. to boost its sagging morale by show of its flag in the Indian Ocean. All this, coupled with the gradual erosion of the British supremacy in the region, tempted the U.S. to don the British mantle. The Ocean which was considered a British lake was attempted to be turned into an American lake.

The Soviet interests in the region have been traced by analysts to Peter the Great and Catherine I and their quest for 'warm water ports'. The above desire was manifest in the secret Molotov-Ribbentrop pact of 1940 whereby Nazi Germany acknowledged an exclusive sphere of Soviet presence and influence in the Indian Ocean area.[37] Within a year of the British withdrawal, the Soviet Union started deploying its naval force in the Indian Ocean. Vietnam, which had been a bastion of American neocolonialism, came under the influence of the Soviet Union. India, according to the Western news media, had agreed to provide certain facilities to the Soviets at Vishakhapatnam and also granted some bunkering and other facilities in the Andamans and Nicobar islands.[38] These reports were unsubstantiated rumours.[39] The presence of the Soviet troops in Afghanistan allegedly enabled Moscow to be at the threshold of realisation of the dream of Peter the Great, i.e., reaching out to the warm waters of the Indian Ocean.

As soon as the British announced their partial tactical withdrawal, the Western media, in order to make a case for the

American penetration of the Indian Ocean region, started giving out stories of Soviet intrusion in the region. The Soviet naval activity was reported to have started with calls by Soviet ships to friendly ports in the area. During the U.S. Seventh Fleet's Task Force's excursion into the Indian Ocean the movement of the Soviet naval vessels was also reported.[40]

Earlier, extensive investigations were reportedly carried out in the Bay of Bengal by the Soviet Union. It was also reported that it gave assistance to Pakistan to develop fishing harbour at Gwadur and to Egypt for building a new fishing port in the Gulf of Suez. Mauritius also entered into an agreement with the Soviet Union on 14 July 1970 providing port facilities to Soviet fishing vessels in return for technical assistance.[41] The West thought that the Soviet vessels were equipped with sensitive devices which would "do a lot of electronic snooping".[42]

The major reason given why the Soviet Union wanted to make its presence felt is its desire to reach the warm waters. But the Soviet Union does have access to ice-free ports of the Mediterranean which it lacked when Peter the Great is supposed to have talked of warm water ports. The Soviet interest in the free navigation across the Indian Ocean and the various entries and exits is understandable, for this is the only route which connects its Far Eastern ports (Vladivostok) and the Eruopean ports (Baltic Sea).[43]

Another reason advanced by some analysts is that Moscow has invested hundreds of millions of dollars in this region in the form of economic and military aid. This kind of reasoning has amplified the meaning of investment. The investment made by the U.S. is understandable because the investment ensures superprofits to the American investors, but Moscow does not have any investment which gives it profits. It has provided aid to various countries for building infrastructural facilities and has also given loans.

T.B. Miller is of the view that Soviet aims include protection of its shipping, development of a capacity to track down and counter American nuclear submarines, the projection of the Soviet political and economic power, denial to the West of the access to resources and the opportunity to pressurise the oil producing countries.[44] Though at present the Soviet Union does not need the West Asian oil as badly as the West does, yet it is interested in protecting its supply for its future needs. Moreover, Moscow wants to maintain the Friendship Pipeline which carries oil from the Ural fields to Poland, East Germany, Czechoslovakia and Hungary.[45] Again, Moscow desires to keep its oil export to Western Europe and Japan to earn hard currency and machinery which could be procured from the West with the oil sale proceeds and "grab the West by the throat".[46] The West Asian oil's cheapness (actual cost $ 200 billion a year) could be manipulated to "influence friends and split hostile alliance".[47] Yet another explanation is that the Red Fleet wants to reduce the offensive power of the Western allies in Europe by forcing them to commit far greater forces to the defence of the sea lanes. Some analysts are of the view that Moscow's desire is to contain China so that it is not able to acquire political influence in the volatile Arab States.

India's response to the presence of the Soviet in the Indian Ocean is less hostile than the one to the U.S. build-up primarily because of two reasons. First, because the Soviet presence is considered defensive and, second, because the Soviet Union has certain responsibilities under the Indo-Soviet Treaty of Friendship, Peace and Cooperation. The Soviet presence in the Indian Ocean is not considered a threat to India; rather it may be helpful to India in case of a threat to India's security as it happened in 1971.

The Sino-Pak axis is another alarming factor as far as India's security is concerned. Though China is not much of a naval power, the Chinese interest in the Indian Ocean cannot be underestimated. It is not for nothing that they have invested money on the Karakoram road system much beyond the expected utility. It appears that apart from spreading a net around Kashmir, its purpose is to have an easy access to the Indian Ocean. Beijing wants to make its presence felt in Africa and West Asia. The Chinese ambiguity on Kashmir dispute and her border agreement with Pakistan should also be viewed in the larger framework of her Afro-Asian and Indian Ocean strategy.

Pakistan had been one of the major littoral countries which had offered bases to the U.S. In return for the U.S. arms Pakistan had been toeing the U.S. line all along. In respect of

Indian Ocean, Pakistan had been blowing hot and cold. It had been expressing lip sympathy with the demand of making the Indian Ocean a Zone of Peace. On the other hand, it supported the American presence in the Indian Ocean. When the whole of the littoral was afire as a result of the establishment of Diego Garcia, Bhutto said in a radio talk that Pakistan had "no objection to the establishment of an American base in the Indian Ocean".[48]

Pakistan has all along been obsessed with India's relatively superior strength and has tried to achieve parity or near parity with it. The parity syndrome had been Pakistan's major foreign policy problem. Moreover, its threat perception and dysfunctional syndrome has been responsible for attracting one of the Super Powers to intrude into the region, thus deteriorating India's security situation.[49] The establishment of a U.S. naval base on Pakistani coast and the visit of U.S. ships carrying nuclear warheads to the Pakistani ports is indeed alarming.

Placed in such a geo-strategic situation India has to revise its strategy. The geo-strategic situation, size and physical configuration of India make it a natural predominant power because these factors are considered favourable for developing into a maritime power of considerable significance. It abuts into the Indian Ocean for almost a thousand miles and virtually dominates it geographically. India has an open coastline of about 2,000 miles and over 90% of her foreign trade is sea-borne. Whosoever controls the Indian Ocean, has not only India's sea-borne trade at its mercy but also her independence. Apart from a long and not very well protected coastline, India has 667 islands (Andamans) in the Bay of Bengal and 588 islands (Lakshdweep) in the Arabian Sea which are highly vulnerable in the face of two strong navies prowling in the neighbourhood.

While to other countries, the Indian Ocean is only one of the important oceanic areas, to India it is the vital sea, her life-line to survival. India has the biggest stakes in its waters. When some hegemonistic attempts are made, India naturally feels perturbed and has to mobilise opinion against making this region a theatre of war or even cold war and seeks cooperation of likeminded countries. India has all along opposed the establishment of foreign military bases. It had opposed them when its neighbours were roped inaggressive military pacts, and had done so when the Americans had leapfrogged into the Indian Ocean.[50] India has all along believed that the U.S. presence would invite Soviet retaliation and the imbroglio would be complete. India's stand on the 'vacuum theory' and the efforts at converting the Indian Ocean into a zone of peace has been in consonance with both the traditions of the anti-colonial struggle and the country's own enlightened self-interest. India hosted an International Conference on the Indian Ocean in 1974 in which the Indian leaders urged an early end to foreign military bases in the Indian Ocean. Swaran Singh, the then Minister of External Affairs, said:

> It is our strong belief that if the declaration is implemented in letter and spirit, resulting in halting of escalation and eventually elimination of great power rivalry in the Indian Ocean, the question of the regional security of the States concerned would find no problem at all. With the removal of the cause itself, the resulting tensions and impediments of peace would diminish and eventually disappear.[51]

India has all along, specially after the movement of the Enterprise on a 'shady enterprise' in the Bay of Bengal in 1971, realised the threat posed to her security by the presence of foreign powers in the Indian Ocean. The U.S. naval action in the Bay of Bengal is a clear example of creating indirect psychological pressures and threats which the U.S. considers as a deterrent. In view of these threats, India has taken steps to meet the challenges to her security. Security has various dimensions, viz. security from - (a) military threats; (b) politico-strategic threats; (c) threat to its economic interests and (d) against psychological pressure. India's strategy should not necessarily be reactive but innovative and should be articulated after a meaningful interaction among all concerned.

It may be recalled that India's defence strategy had so far been north-oriented, i.e., fear of aggression from Pakistan and China dominated the strategic thinking of the Indian leaders. As a result, greater emphasis was laid on defence preparedness in the Himalayas, the Punjab plains and the Rajasthan desert. The real importance of navy was realised after 1971. It may be instructive to point out that when India became independent its navy had just two sloops, two frigates and some harbour defence craft. Over the years India has expanded its defence potential. It has now the eighth largest navy, the third largest army and the fifth largest air force in the world.

REFERENCES

1. Lok Sabha Debates, Series 4, V. 2, April 6, 1967, Cols. 3207-3223.
2. *Ibid.*, also see J.P. Anand, 'Diego Garcia Base'. *IDSA Journal* (New Delhi), Vol. XII, No. 1, July-September, 1979, p. 71.
3. Lok Sabha Debates, Series 4, V. 3, June 22, 1967, Cols. 3040-3049.
4. The concept of 'power vacuum' in the Indian Ocean was first discussed by the study group of the Indian Council of World Affairs. See *Defence and Security in the Indian Ocean Area* (New Delhi, 1958), p. 163; See K.P. Misra, 'International Politics in the Indian Ocean'. *Orbis,* 14(4), Winter 1975, pp. 1000-1108. Also by the same author 'Vacuum of Power in the Indian Ocean,' *Indian Journal of Politics* (Aligarh), Vol. VI, No. 2, August, 1977, pp. 105-110.
5. Quoted from Mrs. Indira Gandhi's address in Colombo, *The Times of India,* April 29, 1973; *Also Indian and Foreign Review* (New Delhi), May 15, 1973, p. 6.
6. Lok Sabha Debates, IV Series, V. 39, April 18, 1970, Cols. 241-45.
7. Bhabani Sen Gupta, Indian Perception of Great Power Presence in Indian Ocean, Allahabad, February, 12-14, 1983, p. 1.
8. Lok Sabha Debates, Vol. 8, November 9, 1970, Col. 247.
9. Foreign Affairs Record, Vol. XVIII, No. II, Nov. 1972, p. 354.
10. *Ibid.*, Vol. XVIII, No. 4, April, 1972, p. 94.
11. Lok Sabha Debates, Vol. XXXVI, No. 15, March 12, 1974, Cols. 187-90.
12. Reply of Atal Behari Vajpayee on February 27, 1978 in Lok Sabha to the calling attention notice by Dr. Baldev, Foreign Affairs Record, Vol. XXIV, No. 2, February, 1978, p. 75.
13. Prime Minister Mrs. Indira Gandhi's views quoted in PKS Namboodri, J.P. Anand and Sreedhar, *Intervention in the Indian Ocean* (New Delhi, 1982), p. 221.
14. 'For us to go ahead and develop a base in the Indian Ocean is an invitation and I will guarantee that they will have a base in the Indian Ocean. So we will be aggressors in this situation....' committee on Foreign relations, United States' Relations with

Communist Countries, 93rd Congress, 2nd Session, August 15, 20 & Sept. 10, 12, 16, 19, 24 and 25 and October 1, 8, 1974 (Washington, D.C.), p. 5.

15. P.V. Narasimha Rao, India's External Affairs Minister, informed Rajya Sabha, see *The Times of India*, March 21, 1982.
16. See *The Times of India*, April 27, 1981; also see Soviet President's 7-point proposal for peace in the Indian Ocean and the Persian Gulf, which he gave while addressing the Indian Parliament on December 10, 1980. See Mikhail Goryanov, *Two Ways of Looking at Indian Ocean* (Moscow, 1981), pp. 52-54.
17. K. Rajendra Singh, *Politics of the Indian Ocean* (New Delhi, 1974), pp. 180-181.
18. *Review of International Affairs* (Belgrade), No. 491, September 21, 1970, pp. 21-23.
19. K.P. Misra, *Quest for an International Order in the Indian Ocean* (Bombay, 1977), pp. 135-38.
20. For the U.S. stand see Text of David Adamson's statement as U.S. Alternative Representative to the Ad Hoc Committee on the Indian Ocean on April 19, 1983 in Backgrounder (USIS, New Delhi), April 29, 1983, pp. 1-13.
21. For detailed discussion see K. Subrahmanyam, 'Indian Ocean as a Zone of Peace', paper in International Seminar on Indian Ocean, Allahabad, February, 1983, pp. 2-6.
22. P.K.S. Namboodri and others, *International Order in the Indian Ocean* (New Delhi, 1982), pp. 226-27.
23. *Indian Express* (New Delhi), July 10, 1980.
24. Ranko Petkovic, 'Colombo's messages-basic thrust of Non-Alignment Action', *Review of International Affairs* (Belgrade), Vol. XXX, No. 701, June 20, 1979, p. 3.
25. K.P. Misra, Quest for an International Order in the Indian Ocean, *op. cit.*, p. 106; Also 'Developments in the Indian Ocean Area, The Littoral Response', *International Studies* (New Delhi), Vol. XVI, No. 1, January-March, 1977.
26. K.R. Singh, *The Indian Ocean : Big Power Presence and Local Response* (New Delhi, 1977), pp. 320-21.
27. P.R. Chari, 'The Indian Ocean : An Indian View Point', *Iranian Review of International Relations* (Teheran) 8, Fall and Autumn, 1976, p. 178.
28. 'India is opposed to a super power naval arms competition in the Indian Ocean..., India is strongly opposed to domination of the ocean by a single world power......India wants Soviet naval presence to balance U.S. naval presence......India cannot rule out Soviet naval support in a future military conflict with Pakistan

or China', Bhabani Sen Gupta, *Soviet-Asian Relations in the 1970s and beyond-an Interperceptional Study,* (New York, 1976), pp. 124-25.

29. Alain Lamballe, 'India and Indian Ocean', *Vikrant* (New Delhi), Vol. VIII, No. 9, June, 1978, p. 24.
30. Jack Spence, 'Naval Armament in the Indian Ocean', in *Sea Power in the 1970s,* ed. by George H. Quester (New York, 1975), p. 133.
31. Baldev Raj Nayar, 'Regional Power in a multipolar world', in *India : A Regional Middle Power,* ed. by John W. Mellor, *op. cit.,* p. 150.
32. Alvin J. Cottrell, 'Indian Ocean of Tomorrow', *Navy Magazine,* March, 1971, p. 10.
33. For a detailed treatment of the latest developments in the field of naval weaponry see R.T. Pretty, 'A Review of the World's Naval Missile Situation' *Navy International,* Vol. 72, 5 May, 1974. For comparative naval fire power of the U.S. and the Soviet Union see Drew Middleton, 'U.S. U.S.S.R., Weapons System', *Dawn,* 9 August, 1978.
34. As cited in K. Subrahmanyam, 'Super Powers in the Indian Ocean Area', (Mimeo) a paper read at a seminar at the India International Centre, 1979.
35. Michael Tanzer, *The Sick Society,* London, 1971, p. 33.
36. Seymour Weiss, 'U.S. Interests and Activities in the Indian Ocean Area', *Department of State Bulletin,* 70 (1815), 8 April, 1974, p. 373.
37. U.S. Department of State, *Nazi-Soviet Relations* 1939-41, Washington, D.C., 1948, p. 250.
38. *The Times* (London), 20 September, 1970.
39. Geoffrey Jukes, 'The Soviet Union and the Indian Ocean', *Survival* (London), November, 1971, pp. 370-71.
40. Surendra Chopra, 'U.S. Foreign Policy Interests in Kashmir', *Indian Journal of Political Studies,* Vol. 2, No. 2, 1978, p. 141.
41. IDSA, India in World Strategic Environment : Annual Review, Vol.2, New Delhi, 1973, p. 703.
42. *Hong Kong Standard,* 27 July, 1970.
43. Anthony Harrigan, 'The Indian Ocean and U.S. Security', *Vital Speeches of the Day,* p. 674.
44. Cited in Anthony Harrigan, *op. cit.*
45. M.S. Agwani, *Politics in the Gulf,* New Delhi, 1978, pp. 131-33.
46. John C. Campbell, 'Middle East Oil : American Policy and Super Power Interaction', *Survival,* Vol. 15, No. 5, September-October, 1973, p. 217.

47. Shahram Chubin, 'U.S. Security in the Persian Gulf in the 1980s', *Deadalus*, Fall, 1980, pp. 46-47.
48. *Pakistan Times*, 27 April, 1974.
49. Surendra Chopra, 'India-Pakistan Relations', in Pandav Naik, ed., *Pakistan : Society and Politics,* Delhi, 1984, pp. 212-239.
50. Surendra Chopra, 'Pakistan, Pacts and Kashmir', *Indian Journal of Political Science,* Vol. 25, No. 4, 1965.
51. Lok Sabha Debates, Series 5, Vol. 36, 12 March, 1974, Cols. 172-193.

CHAPTER V

Politics of a 'Zone of Peace'

The Indian Ocean and Politics of Peace Zone

A study of the proposal for Peace Zone in the Indian Ocean reveals how the basic variables of any proposal can be moulded from a simple to a complex structure by using the tools of diplomacy, including conference diplomacy. Several regional powers have, willingly or unwillingly, been a party to this game. The result is that their concerted demand for the creation of a Peace Zone in the Indian Ocean has been brushed aside. Not only has the original 1971 General Assembly resolution been side-tracked and new variables sought to be legitimized through the Indian Ocean meeting in New York in 1979, but the U.N. Conference on the Indian Ocean, which was to be held in Colombo, has been postponed year after year. The concept of a Peace Zone in the Indian Ocean (PZIO) has reached the rock bottom level in terms of its implementation.

The main thrust of the Great Power diplomacy has been to try to equate the factors that lead to the destabilization in the Indian Ocean, because of the Great Power presence, with the tensions among the littoral States, and the removal of the first, conditional upon the second. In other words, these non-regional powers have sought, and to some extent obtained, legitimacy for their own actions. The concept of consensus and membership of the Great Powers in the Ad Hoc Committee of the Indian Ocean gives them a virtual 'veto' on matters pertaining to the creation of a Peace Zone in the Indian Ocean. Several regional powers have indirectly promoted such a situation. They have also accepted those formulations as is seen from the resolution approved by them in New York in 1979. Thus, the elimination of nuclear weapons of the Great Powers from the Indian Ocean has been linked with the acceptance of full-scope nuclear safeguard, and reduction of Great Power military presence by balanced force reduction among the regional powers. Regional rivalry has been equated with the Cold War rivalry. Even the concept of freedom of navigation has been twisted to mean the right to station force in far away regions under the garb of protecting sea lanes even in peace times.

The period of two decades, 1964-1984, which saw the rise and the decline of the Peace Zone concept can be divided into three main parts : the gathering of strength, the erosion of strength, and the dilution of the concept. With the 'veto' powers of Great Powers in the Ad Hoc Committee and the near impossibility of convening the conference on the Indian Ocean, it is possible that the concept itself may finally wither away.

The concept began to gain strength after 1964 when Mrs. Bandaranaike pronounded it at the Non-aligned Conference at Cairo. Great Power interest in the Indian Ocean was manifest through a series of events between 1963-1964; the dispatch of the U.S. task force to the Indian Ocean, the successful trials of the A-3 Polaris missile, the decision to construct the Very Low Frequency (VLF) communication centre at North West Cape and the carving out of the island groups to create a new political entity called the British Indian Ocean Territory (BIOT).

The Anglo-American negotiations on Diego Garcia base highlighted the growing militarization of the Indian Ocean area in the context of Great Power rivalry. India, as one of the leading non-aligned States in the area, drew international attention towards that development. It was obvious even from newspaper reports that the British were reviewing their defence policy in the light of their dwindling economic resources and the primacy given to the NATO. Thus, the gradual withdrawal from the position east of the Suez was no surprise. In fact, the carving out of the BIOT, the negotiations on Diego Garcia, the dispatch of U.S. taskforce and the decision to strengthen Iran as a local surrogate appeared to be a part of the anticipated withdrawal. The decision announced in 1968 to withdraw from the east of Suez was an acceptance of the reality and also a formal notice of the direction of British policy in the years to come.

It was an interesting coincidence that the British announcement in January 1968 was followed by the formal entry of the Soviet taskforce in the Indian Ocean. It was in response to the series of events like the successful firing of Polaris A-3 missile, the construction of the VLF communication base in N.W. Cape in Australia, the completion of the Anglo-American negotiations on Diego Garcia and the periodic visits of the U.S. taskforce to the Indian Ocean. The decision to send the Soviet task force also followed the closure of the Suez Canal after the June 1967 War, thereby depriving the Soviets of the shortest sea-route to the area.

It is important to note that the West did not take the entry of the Soviet taskforce or its possibility seriously. Britain not only granted independence to Aden Protectorate (South Yemen) knowing fully well the radical orientation of its elite and their linkages with Egypt and the USSR but also disbanded its major naval base in Aden in November 1967. The entry of the Soviet taskforce also did not alter the British policy of withdrawal from the east of Suez. If the West was so concerned by the entry of the Soviet taskforce, it could have delayed the formal British withdrawal or made suitable alternative arrangements. But the Nixon Doctrine of September 1969 almost ignored the area and left its 'defence' to the willingness of the local powers. However, the presence of the Soviet taskforce was subsequently made an excuse to further strengthen the U.S. presence especially in the context of the energy crisis after 1972.

The Non-Aligned Movement, however, took the growing Great Power presence in the Indian Ocean seriously and saw it as a source of future threat to the security of the region. It not only criticised the Diego Garcia base but also sought a halt to the growing Great Power presence in the area. Those regional powers, which were linked directly or indirectly with these Great Powers, did not raise their voice against these developments. Only the Non-Aligned Movement (NAM) took up that question and discussed it in detail at the Lusaka Summit in September 1970. It not only defined the concept of Peace Zone in the Indian Ocean (PZIO) but also incorporated it in its final declaration. Subsequently, these States introduced it as an item in the U.N. General Assembly and succeeded in getting it passed as Resolution 2832 (XXVI) in December 1971. Several of the regional powers which were aligned to one Great Power or the other voted against it at that time.

The item continued to be presented in the General Assembly and gradually the number of countries voting in favour of the resolution increased. By 1974, almost all the littoral States had voted for it. The sudden decline of alliance popularity and the growing Arab hostility towards the USA following the October War were partly responsible for these votes. The General Assembly also created in 1972 an Ad Hoc Committee on the Indian Ocean. Over a number of years, its membership increased with the result that the composition of that committee began to change drastically. The non-aligned States that had introduced the resolution in 1971 began to be overshadowed by those which had earlier voted against it or those which had an axe to grind. Gradually, the Ad Hoc Committee became a useful tool of Great Power diplomacy and was used to change the very ethos of the Peace Zone proposal.

The most important diplomatic move that undermined the concept of PZIO, as reflected in the 1971 Resolution of the General Assembly, was the contention of the Great Powers that it was conditional upon the prior implementation of all these conditions, that were meant for the Great Powers, by the littoral States themselves. Once that principle was conceded to, instruments were found to undermine the NAM's solidarity and its concept of PZIO.

Three concepts, that were not there in the 1971 Resolution, were subsequently added to the PZIO basket; nuclear weapon free zones in the littoral regions of the Indian Ocean; mutual arms reduction among the regional powers; and a built-in mechanism for ensuring regional peace and for conflict resolution. India raised serious reservations on these newly added concepts, especially when attempts were made to impose them upon her within the limited geographical framework of the Indian sub-continent or South Asia. Since India was a major motive force behind the concept of PZIO, these tools were used to present India as the main hurdle in the process of evolving PZIO. Gradually, after 1974, the emphasis of the discussion on PZIO shifted from the activities of the Great Powers and the global issues affecting peace and security of the Indian Ocean to regional issues. The littoral States themselves were accused of undermining peace and security in the region.

The concept of Nuclear Weapon Free Zone (NWFZ) in the Indian Ocean was made conditional upon the acceptance of full-scope safeguards by the littoral powers. India, which had developed an independent nuclear technology, was selected as the main target. India had serious reservations about the imposition of the NWFZ in South Asia by outside powers. Moreover, the Indian leadership had given repeated assurances that it was developing its nuclear capability for peaceful use only. Yet a lot of hue and cry was raised since 1974 that it was India and not the Great Powers that stood in the way of elimination of nuclear weapons from the Indian Ocean. On the contrary, those Great Powers, which are capable of deploying nuclear weapons in the Indian Ocean area, did not give any assurance of their non-use in the region. The only concession that they were prepared to offer was that if the regional powers agreed on a full-scope safeguard they would not be the primary target of their nuclear strike.

It did not come as a surprise when some of those Great Powers that were so vehement on imposing nuclear safeguard on India voted against similar resolutions in the General Assembly when the question of imposing full-scope safeguard on South Africa and Israel was raised in the General Assembly in December 1981 within the framework of NWFZ in Africa and the Middle East respectively. In the case of South Africa (General Assembly Resolution 36/86), USA, UK, France and Israel, voted against the resolution. In the case of Israel (Resolution 36/87) only USA and Israel put negative votes. Thus, some of these Great Powers voted against their own stand, the concept of regional NWFZ, in two areas while seeking to support it in South Asia. Reasons for their support for South Africa and Israel and opposition to India are too obvious.

Indian opposition to the concept of NWFZ, is based on several grounds. First, it is discriminatory. It divides the world into two groups: the nuclear haves and the have-nots. In that world, only the haves would have the right to own nuclear weapons and, therefore, to fight a nuclear war. One reason advocated for denying it to the have-nots is that they are not to be trusted. No adequate reason is given except that they are irresponsible. In other words, by their definition, the possession of nuclear weapons is the hall-mark of responsibility within the framework of present world order. The second argument advanced for the benefit of the have-nots is that if they surrender the control their nuclear technology to the haves, they would be given political guarantees that would save them from a nuclear devastation even if the haves do fight a nuclear war.

Both arguments are not only illogical but also wrong on facts. The exclusive club of the haves has been constantly infiltrated. Earlier, France and China joined it. Now, South Africa and Israel have attained that membership though it is not accepted publicly. Soon, others will join it despite the opposition. It is a technological achievement that is not beyond the reach of several developing countries. Thus, the so-called exclusiveness of the nuclear club is factually incorrect. Secondly, the guarantee about the have nots remaining unaffected in a nuclear conflict is not worth the paper on which it is written.

Many in India question the very rationale of creating NWFZs in various regions of the Third World. The dangers arising out of the proliferation of nuclear weapons has to be seen in its global and not regional or subregional context. The concept of NWFZ in different regions would only drag the people of the Third World into serious nuclear danger. The acceptance of the concept of NWFZs in the Third World alone would mean that they have accepted the concept of nuclear weapon zones and, ipso facto, of nuclear war zones. Thus, nuclear threat to the world cannot be contained by creating NWFZs in the Third World, whose countries do not have the capability to destroy the world. It can be best averted only by halting all types of nuclear proliferation and by projecting the concept of NWFZ at the global level. Like the issue of NWFZ in South Asia, the question of balance force reduction and the creation of a framework for regional peace and security in South Asia were also projected in and outside the U.N. as of vital importance for the creation of PZIO. The Persian Gulf, arms were pouring in and tension rising beyond proportion, was not highlighted. The Saudis and the Shah of Iran could not be touched.

The proposals mentioned above were debated and incorporated in the Final Declaration of the Meeting of Littoral and Hinterland States of the Indian Ocean in New York, and were accepted by the General Assembly in its Resolution 34/80 of 11 December 1979. After elaborating what the Great Powers should do to create PZIO, it says, "Considering also that the creation of a Zone of Peace in the Indian Ocean requires cooperating among the regional States to ensure conditions of peace and security within the region, as envisaged in the Declaration, and the sovereignty and territorial integrity of the littoral and hinterland States." The Great Powers and the Indian Ocean States were equated as far as the PZIO was concerned. Thus the acceptance of PZIO by Great Powers was made conditional, inter alia, upon cooperation among regional powers. During the debates in the preceding years, several States like Indonesia, Pakistan and Sri Lanka clearly sought to establish a linkage between the threat to regional peace by Great Powers rivalry and by regional rivalry and indirectly attempted to make the elimination of Great Power presence conditional upon the establishment of regional mechanism acceptable to all. Such was never the intention of those who had propounded the concept of PZIO in the late sixties and the early seventies.

The erosion of the peace zone concept coincided with the increase in the Great Power presence in the area. This was mainly in two phases. The first phase began with the so-called 'energy crisis' scenerio as propounded in the USA in 1971-72, followed by the oil crisis of 1973-74. This phase was used to justify the dispatch of powerful taskforces to the region, open threat by the USA to occupy the oil fields and the launching of the second phase of the expansion of the Diego Garcia base. The Soviet base in Somalia came as useful additional argument to justify that expansion. The ouster of the Soviets from Somalia was ignored subsequently when dealing with Diego Garcia base.

The second phase in 1978-79 coincided with the beginning of the new Cold War, the ouster of the USSR from Somalia, the breaking of the US-USSR talks on the Indian Ocean and the destabilization in Iran. Once again the response was similar;

dispatch of large taskforce, renewed threat to occupy the oil fields and the activization of the plans for the rapid deployment force (RDF). The crucial 1979 debate in the U.N. on the Indian Ocean coincided with that phase. Subsequently, the Soviet military intervention in Afghanistan and the Iraq-Iran War added more arguments to justify the plans for an enhanced Western presence in the region. Thus, the concept of PZIO was further eroded by massive preparations by Great Powers to convert the Indian Ocean into a war zone with the active collaboration of some of those very littoral States that had earlier voted for the Peace Zone proposal.

Despite concerted efforts to undermine the original concept of PZIO and to postpone its implementation, there is a growing urgency for the creation of a Peace Zone in the Indian Ocean. Unfortunately, attempts have been made over the years not only to add new points to the original package but also to make the acceptance of the old and the new mutually conditional. Hence, all efforts to reach a package deal have failed so far and there is no possible way to reconcile all these conditions. Yet, there is great urgency to break this impasse. One alternative is to break the package into components and to try to seek solution to those at different levels. In fact, the Ad Hoc Committee and the General Assembly partly accepted this method when they welcomed the US-USSR talks on the Indian Ocean. Though the talks broke down in 1978, the General Assembly in its resolution of 1979 urged the USA and the USSR to resume their talks regarding their military presence in the Indian Ocean.

The package of PZIO, as it is constituted today, can be sub-divided into five more or less independent variables in the sense that the fulfilment of one is not necessarily dependent upon that of the other. In other words, if efforts are made to work out a solution of these variables even independently, the total effort would amount to achieving PZIO in easy stages. These five main variables are:

(i) Great Power rivalry in the context of the Cold War, especially regarding the deployment of the strategic-nuclear weapon systems.

(ii) The question of denuclearization, especially when perceived from the point of view of the nuclear-weapon powers and the non-nuclear weapon powers. Such a difference in perception is also reflected in the global versus regional approach to the question of denuclearization.

(iii) Great Power interest in the region, the linkage between regional and non-regional powers and its possible impact on regional security.

(iv) The need to evolve a non-aligned security doctrine which can present an alternative to the existing doctrines based upon the use of force and the inevitability of conflict.

(v) Lastly, to be effective, especially while bargaining with Great Powers, the non-aligned States, singly or collectively, must demonstrate their capability to fulfil their obligation towards the international community. Unless they are able to do this, others would not only ignore them but also feel free to take such actions as they might deem appropriate to safeguard their national interests.

It should not be forgotten that the concept of PZIO was advocated by the NAM as an alternative to the growing Cold War rivalry in the Indian Ocean. Unfortunately, soon after 1973, the main thrust of the NAM was gradually replaced by the syndrome of the Cold War conflict, something which the NAM wanted to avoid. The result is that the concept of PZIO has itself become a tool of the Cold War conflict and Great Power diplomacy. The NAM has, therefore, to evolve a more appropriate strategy and a framework of operation to set the movement for PZIO on the right course.

Indian Ocean Islands: Case for a Security Framework

There exists a certain security dimension in the relationship between the island republics in the Indian Ocean. This dimension has so far remained unexplored. This should not only be explored and emphasised upon but also put within a framework—explicit or implicit.

One of the manifestations of the Indian Ocean power rivalry has been the establishment of a permanent naval/air support base like the Diego Garcia in the heart of the Indian

Ocean itself and also 'facilities', 'accesses' and other non-descriptive 'host nations, support'. For considerations of geopolitics and natural resources, the north-western littoral of the Indian Ocean has remained the focus of military build-up in recent years. There are, in fact, signs to suggest that a military thrust towards the Ocean itself may not be far too long to exploit its emerging strategic potential.

The traditional U.S. concerns in the region have been the security of oil lanes, protection of economic and political investments, stability of allies and friends and prevention of a seaward thrust of the Soviet Union. These objectives were sought to have been secured by essentially building the regional infrastructure for a swift and decisive U.S. military action to forestall threats to the American interests. All or some of these assumptions may remain valid for future as well. However, besides these basically land-based politico-military and economic interests, new sea-based strategic concerns have emerged recently which for the United States would prove to be far more significant in its global competition than those centering around the South-West Asian region.

First, the U.S. strategists have begun to see great advantage in exploiting the vulnerability of the Soviet land power by confronting it from the open seafront of the Indian Ocean. This at once puts the Soviet Union on the defensive. Not only that it also stems the perceived Soviet push towards the warm waters of the Indian Ocean thereby keeping the Soviet navy in its present bottled-up status of dependency on well-monitored international waterways for its entry into the oceans.

Secondly, the Indian Ocean could become in future an ideal deployment area for the American nuclear missile submarines. Nuclear war strategy demands survivability of the second-strike capability based on submarines. This can best be achieved by dispersing the force in all the oceans. The Atlantic and the Pacific have already become high density anti-submarine warfare theatres and hence less assured survivability. Moreover, the US nuclear submarines in the Indian Ocean are in a better position to target Soviet military and industrial centres from their sanctuaries in the Indian Ocean. Its peculiar geographical features would either neutralise of at least diffuse Soviet air defence systems.

Thirdly, in another context of nuclear warfare also, the Indian Ocean has a role to play. Though no one knows how exactly an atomic war would be conducted, strategists visualise it to begin with an all-out attack on the adversary's satellites which perform the command, control, communication and intelligence functions which are vital for the conduct of the war. This attack to blind the enemy will be simultaneous and orchestrated in such a fashion as to hit and destroy all of them, including stand bys, in one single stroke. Anti-satellite missiles have been tested and it is believed that such missiles launched from carrier-borne aircrafts in the Indian Ocean would be an essential part of the anti-satellite weaponry. Satellites employed in this mission in their elliptical orbit will be closest to the earth over the Indian Ocean and hence more vulnerable to attack.

Fourthly, one of the hypotheses in President Reagan's Strategic Defence Initiative or 'Star Wars' is to destroy Soviet missiles in their boost phase by directing high energy laser beams on to them from space based systems. The energy for this is provided by a nuclear explosion in space carried out by one's own 'prop up' missiles launched from submarines, presumably also from relatively safe havens of the Indian Ocean.

Therefore, even if other interests like oil etc. cease to be matters of extreme concern in future, the geostrategic disposition of the Indian Ocean alone is sufficient to ensure the abiding strategic interest of the United States.

Similarly, the Soviet Union is reportedly building its new class of 60,000 tons submarines with titanium hull. The USSR is also building its first conventional nuclear-powered aircraft carriers. The likely deployment of these is projected to take place in the Indian Ocean. Logically, the Chinese nuclear missile submarines now under construction may also find their deployment areas in the north-western part of the Indian Ocean, targeted on the Soviet Union.

The interplay of strategic forces of global powers in the waters around the Indian subcontinent is thus not a farfetched propsect - it is, in fact, almost certain. Recent reports say that the U.S. is planning to set up an ELF (Extremely Low Frequency) station in Sri Lanka, the purpose of which is specifically to communicate with submerged nuclear submarines. An electronic telescope, a segment of the 'spacetrack' programme of the U.S. which is meant to serve the 'Star Wars' plans, has already come up on Diego Garcia.

It is also certain that the littoral States, and more particularly the islands in the Indian Ocean, will come under increasing pressure of external powers for infrastructural support needed for their massive military deployment in the region. If this scenario is accepted even partly, the Indian concern to promote a secure environment in its oceanic neighbourhood has to envisage a role for India in the security and stability of some of the important island groups.

Small States have a different set of security concerns than the middle-sized and larger ones. In the case of small islands their feeling of vulnerability is compounded because of their isolation. New means of intervention have further exposed their vulnerability. The accompanying Table portrays a broad picture of the unique nature of the security problems faced by these islands and their almost non-existent resources to face challenges. A comparison with the Indian situation will help understand it better. The combined profile of all the three islands together represents, both in terms of area and population, a Goa with less land but a little more population. Their combined GNP is less than a billion dollars, or one-sixth of annual Indian defence spending. Their net inflow of external resources is a little more than India's total allocation for aid to another countries.

The striking feature of the security of these islands is their obvious vulnerability to both carrots and sticks of the big powers who would want to get a foothold in the Indian Ocean. Economically, they are dependent largely on a single source like fisheries in Maldives, sugarcane in Mauritius and tourism in Seychelles, though efforts are on to diversify their economies. They all have large trade deficits which is balanced by a steady flow of external aid which constitutes a significant chunk of their total resources.

Table

A Statistical Profile of Indian Ocean Islands

	Items	*Maldives*	*Mauritius*	*Seychelles*
1.	Area (sq. km.)	298	1,865	404
2.	No. of Islands	2,000	4	92
3.	Uninhabited Islands	1,780	-	n.a
4.	Population	1,43,000	9,25,000	62,000
5.	GNP ($mn)	n.a.	800	100
6.	External Trade:			
	Exports (Rs. crores)	4	243	10
	Imports (Rs. crores)	13	363	40
7.	External Aid ($ mn Annual)	6.5	600	18
8.	Defence Force	n.a.	4,000	800
9.	Bases of Military significance (in existence)	Gan	Diego Gercia	Mahe

Secondly, though strategically important and under constant threats of various sorts, they hardly possess any defence capability. As a result, either they remain exposed to external intervention or they have to seek security guarantees or try to countervail one power against the other.

A full-scale armed invasion by a global power, though not ruled out, is not the kind of threat to stability and security faced by these islands. The attempts in the past have been to change the regimes by subtle means of organising a coup or sending in mercenaries to overthrow the governments.

President Rene has repeatedly stated that he would not give military bases to big powers of either Eastern or Western bloc. Explaining the dilemma Seychells faces, he said : 'But our problem is our strategic position. Both Super Powers believe that the other will not permit us to be non-aligned and that we will not be firm enough to remain non-aligned'. This in essence is the problem faced by other islands in the Indian Ocean as well.

In the distant Comoros, another Indian Ocean islands group, President Ali Solilih was deposed in May 1978 in a coupled by a European mercenary, Bob Denard, with only 60 others. The ousted government had threatened to wage an armed struggle to liberate Mayotte from French colonial rule.

The former President of Maldives, Ibrahim Nazir, in exile in Singapore hired European mercenaries including former members of Britain's crack Special Air Services (SAS), and made an attempt to capture power in April 1980. The Mauritian leader Ramgoolam once accused Cuba of 'training Mauritian youth in violence and subversive methods', by Cubans stationed in Malagasy. *The Mauritius Times* succinctly put the security dilemma thus: "The strategic position of a country is usually coveted by Super Powers......It would be sheer folly to dismiss the likelihood of a coup in Mauritius. If any, it will be as usual designed by foreign powers".

India's Response

In the 1960s India appeared to have shown greater sensitivity to the militarisation of the Indian Ocean and its impact on the country's security. The Parliamentary debates of that time show that the Members were apprehending far-reaching consequences as a result of the establishment of the BIOT. In June 1967, the then Foreign Minister, M.C. Chagla conveyed to an agitated Parliament the British assurance that the islands it detached from Mauritius and Seychelles would not be used as military bases. Chagla told the House: "We were informed in 1965 by the United Kingdom that they were proposing to buy these islands. At that time we protested and we said it was contrary to the U.N. Resolution. They have given us categoric assurance that these islands will not be used as military bases".

However, in the 1970s and subsequently when large-scale militarisation of the Ocean began, India did not seem to have devised any policy initiatives to meet the security concerns of the islands to ensure that they do not fall under the influence of one or the other power. The Indian policy has, by and large, been content with a diplomatic cum economic response to issues of security concerns to both India and its island neighbours like support to the Mauritian demand for the return of Diego Garcia or the Seychelles demand for a U.N. investigation to the menace of mercenaries.

Of late, India has initiated a modest level of military cooperation with the Seychelles supplying helicopters and offering to train pilot and aircraft technicians. A substantial sum of aid has also been extended. For the first time, an Indian naval ship visited Seychelles in June 1984. An Indian ship also visited Malagassy the same year. Regular Indian ship visits have been taking place to Mauritius. Despite pressures and a reported offer of $ 1 m annual rent, India pursuaded Maldives not to give out Gan airfield to foreign powers and instead to convert it into a tourist place.

While these could be taken as initial steps in the right direction, there is still a wide scope for strengthening the bonds of common security interests between the island republics and India. During her 1982 visit to Mauritius, Mrs. Gandhi was asked whether India would go to the help of Seychelles if there was trouble again. Her reply was: "we sympathise with Seychelles, but we don't think it would be wise for us to get involved in military intervention". On another occasion during the same visit she added: "We are not very strong and, therefore, the possibility of doing much is not very obvious".

India's reluctance to assume the role of a protector and its own self-image of not being adequately strong enough to undertake such a task has to be matched with the perceptions of the leaders of the islands to bring out the contrast. The Seychelles President Rene told an interviewer in 1984: "India would like to play a big role, but it has a complex that people will say they are being imperialistic". Rene said that Seychelles would welcome Indian intervention in the event of future coup attempts against his regime: "India should say, 'we are not going to stand by and let that sort of nonsense go on'. That would deter the adventurers. The Soviet Union says it. This is a role that India could play".

Similar views have been expressed by Mauritian leaders also. An important leader of the ruling Mauritian Socialist Movement, Harish Boodhoo said : "As a littoral country, everyone would wish India to become a power. History has shown that India has no paternal or hegemonistic attitude". Another leader, Sir Satcam Boolel, former Deputy Prime Minister, said, "Indian naval facilities would definitely be accepted by Mauritius, and if they say otherwise, they are merely being diplomatic".

The immediate issue is certainly not the establishment of Indian naval facilities in the islands. It should, however, be made clear that India has sufficient security interests in those islands and that India would counter any attempts to create instability. This message has to be conveyed explicitly by a sufficiently advertised military and intelligence cooperation with the governments in these islands.

India's present and projected naval capability is inadequate to reach help to these islands in case of sudden trouble. Even reaching Maldives is not easy, let alone Mauritius and Seychelles. But if the Indian security planners do give adequate weight to the stability and security of the Indian Ocean islands as being matters of great relevance to India's security, ways can be found to improve India's security interaction with them by providing training, by supplying communication and military equipment and by improving information exchange. Now that India is entering the age of satellites, she should be able to upgrade information on the Indian Ocean region. In the long run, some limited strategic mobility for India forced to go to the rescue of these islands may have to be planned for.

The Indian Ocean As A Zone of Peace : Problems and Prospects

The unduly prolonged failure to implement the resolution passed by the United Nations in December 1971 declaring the Indian Ocean as a Zone of Peace and free from big power military competition has been causing serious anxiety and uncertainty about the peace and development in the Indian Ocean Region, has assumed greater significance for international peace, security and development. The continuous but alarming increase of external militarism in regional affairs has gradually faded the hopes and aspirations of the supporters of the peace zone concept. However, efforts at various levels have resulted in the signing of numerous bilateral and multilateral agreements and declarations, though of limited effect due to lack of pragmatism.

The concept of a Peace Zone as it is generally understood relates to pacification or appeasement. It is governed by two consistently divergent shades; one signifying a condition referring to the absence of turmoil, tension, conflict and war, while the other refers to peace achieved through good management, orderly resolution of conflict and the establishment of harmony and tranquility through understanding and negotiations. However, littoral States act contrary to their determination 'to preserve their independence, sovereignty and territorial integrity, through resolving their political, economic and social problems under conditions of peace and tranquility'. It is believed that it would have been perceived by the promoters of the concept that the absence of clash of interests in the community of nations as an essential condition of peace would be highly unpragmatic. That is why stress has been laid not on the obliteration of the clash of interests but on the resolving of conflict through mutual negotiations and understanding. No doubt, it is not an easy process.

The most difficult problem is created by the involvement of the external powers in the regional affairs. To pursuade them in favour of elimination of competition and mutual rivalries in the Indian Ocean region, as they are harmful to both the regional and the external nations, is in itself a Herculean task. It depends largely in evolving a collective effort by the regional States. The consequent problem, therefore, is how best the regional States can be convinced and pursuaded to accept the phenomenon of collective security of the region.

As the concept of a Peace Zone in the Indian Ocean has wide ramifications, it would be unwise to presume that it can be achieved by exterminating the external powers. Even if the external powers agree to withdraw from the region, the regional problems and differences would continue to pose unsurmountable challenges to the peace in the region. Some of the smaller and weaker States of the Indian Ocean region suspect the bigger and stronger States of the area in the context of their own security and development. On account of their militarist attitude and refusal to solve their problems through negotiations they find an easy alternative in welcoming the presence of the Super Powers in the region rather than having an agreement with the bigger States on equal terms. The eagerness of some of the newly liberated States to invite the military interventionism of the external powers has added a new dimension to the complexity of the problem of peace. The irony of the situation, therefore, is that regional powers are supporting the concept of Peace Zone on the one hand and are concentrating on their military build-up on the other, which is bound to encourage a scramble for dominance within region.

Despite the geographic homogeneity of the region, the relationship among the States of the Indian Ocean presents a kaleidoscopic structure. In view of this, the future of the regional cooperation would continue to be bilateral or sub-regional which in a situation of conflict or crisis is bound to be influenced by the external military presence in the region. The concept of a Peace Zone "calls upon the littoral and hinterland States of the Indian Ocean, the permanent members of the Security Council and other major maritime users of the Indian Ocean, in pursuit of the objectives of establishing a system of universal collective security without military alliances and strengthening international security through regional and other cooperation, to enter into consultations. But the vagueness regarding the procedure to be adopted for consultations has reduced the chances of success and has made the concept a mere wish on the part of a group of Afro-Asian countries, and the resolution adopted in the United Nations, as much as a statement of intent".[1]

The external powers, especially the Super Powers, make the issue further complicated by their criticism that the purpose of the concept amounts to a gross-transgression of the freedom of the seas and the prevailing customary and conventional international laws of the seas. The Big Powers contend that "a group of States in any region cannot establish separate legal regime for the high seas in the region".[2] They also apprehend that the acceptance of such a proposal would curtail their navigational, trade and fishing activities and hinder installation of submerged cables and pipelines, along with the overflights, and would threaten their international security arrangements in the region.

Despite the increasing support to the concept of Peace Zone in the Indian Ocean, the difficulty of acting upon its objectives has remained an elusive problem which tends to increase scepticism in certain diplomatic circles that the concept is both impracticable and unworkable. Some experts also feel that the

U.N. treatment of the issue of Peace Zone concept is marked by "over-simplification, misrepresentation, euphemism and cant".[3] It has also been blamed to lack clarity regarding the curbing of oceanic movements. While referring to the doctrine of the freedom of seas which provides the right of free passage through the international waters, the concept helplessly hopes that "the freedom of the seas will be subject to important voluntary limitations".[4] To substantiate it further, the concept appears to follow a self-contradictory path as, trade on one side, it declared that warships and military aircraft should not be allowed to use the ocean "for any threat or use of force against the sovereignty, territorial integrity, or independence (of the regional countries) in contravention of the purpose and principles of the Charter of the United Nations", while at the same time it refers to "the right to free and unimpeded use of the zone by the vessels of all the nations is unaffected". Such a freedom cannot be absolute.

The problem has been further complicated by the reluctance of the big powers and other maritime users of the Indian Ocean in favour of the resolution which amount to putting the cart before the horse and making it ineffective in its implementation. It has encouraged some of the smaller States to adopt hostile or apathetic attitude towards the concept while convincing the others to consider it too ambitious and premature.

So, the problem of resolving differences among the countries of the Indian ocean regarding the modus operandi to establish a Peace Zone in the region tends to add new dimensions to the problem detracking the main issues. For instance, the proposal of creating a nuclear free zone in South Asia has been diplomatically put forward as a major issue by some States having vested interests. Similarly, some States have suggested the concept of mutual balance of forces among the great powers as an alternative to the concept of Peace Zone in the Indian Ocean because they feel that the great powers would not "let the Indian Ocean be isolated from the global contest for power, influence and security".[5]

The formula of limited balance of forces is not acceptable either to the big powers or the littoral States of the Indian Ocean. The big powers fear that it would act not only as a "constraint upon their activities in the area but would also become a precedent for other oceans as well".[6] The dilemma faced by the Indian Ocean countries is that they cannot accept the outside military presence in the region as it affects the regional development; they cannot also force the outside powers to vacate the area, and their consent to a limited military presence of outside powers would only legitimise it.

The failure of the resolution has also been linked with the inappropriate timing of the meeting which took place in the autumn of 1971 when there was a war on in the Indian subcontinent, a circumstance hardly conducive to appreciate the other country's point of view. Under these circumstances the elimination "from the Indian Ocean of all bases, military installations, logistical supply facilities, the disposition of nuclear weapons and the weapons of mass destruction and manifestations" would not have been feasible.

A major pre-condition in the resolution pertains to the adoption of the principle of de-nuclearisation which is not acceptable to some of the developing nations like India as it allows the external powers to retain, rather develop further, their nuclear potential but prohibits the regional States to do so. Moreover, the problem of disarmament and nuclear weapons pertains to all States of the world, and, therefore, cannot be settled at the regional levels".[7] Therefore, there is an immediate need to clearly define the concept explaining the modus vivendi for its implementation so that the regional and external powers may be pursuaded to reach an understanding or agreement.

In practical terms, the concept has two main dimensions. One, that of the regional States whose immediate concern is security and economic survival. Their vision of world peace does not transcend the regional barriers because they are not developed enough to have a global view of the problem. The other dimension is that regional peace is a step towards global peace. In this case, the Peace Zone concept becomes subservient to the latter. Therefore, the concept of Peace Zone in the Indian Ocean is inseparable from global peace and unrealizable till global peace is established.

The future of the Peace Zone concept depends more on the extent of confidence and cooperation among the regional States.

The creation of a public opinion in favour of the concept would help in keeping it alive. There is also a strong feeling that the regional States should collectively dissociate themselves politically with all those powers which insist on external military presence in the Indian Ocean. It is also suggested that the regional powers by creating adverse situation can force the uncompromising outside powers to reduce their involvement in the regional affairs. The post-World War II history is most relevant to understand the significance of peace because it left the world community shaken and broken by the enormous damage, the maiming and loss of lives which created a desire for the establishment of perennial peace. Even then, the efforts made by certain agencies and leaders could not prove successful in creating an atmosphere free from tensions and conflicts. Although no major war engulfing the whole world has taken place since then, there have been serious regional conflicts. Quite a few of them have brought the world community nearer to the precipice of a world war. If such a war has not taken place so far, much of the credit goes to the fear of unprecedented destruction and not to the move for peace. Such a period of uncertain peace depends on the whims of nations possessing nuclear arms and on the individuals holding reins of power in the big and powerful countries. The ramifications of such a catastrophe would not spare even the coming generations from the devastating effects of destruction. In the light of these developments, it would not be hyperbolic to presume that the world is dangerously sitting on the destructive stockpiles of nuclear armaments, more so when peace is based on the theory of deterrence aimed at mutual annihilation through increased war potentialities. Such a policy, no doubt, ensures peace which is "short-termed, elusive and slippery".[8] It is bound to either break down at any moment or with the passage of time would cease to deter, thereby justifying the apprehension that "arms control is relevant when tension is at a certain point above which it is impossible and beneath which it unnecessary".[9] The realization of the concept of a Peace Zone involves two significant factors. One, the promotion of cordial relations among the regional nations irrespective of their might and influence on corporate basis as equal partners, and two, the creation of conditions for the exit of external military presence from the region. The second factor is feared to be intensifying the Cold War politics. Actually "what frightens the littoral States more is the immediate prospect of conventional naval arms race and the potential conflicts which are likely to arise"[10] from the external powers' rivalry in the region. Under the existing scenario of international political developments, especially the growing tensions in the Indian Ocean region, the realization of the concept of peace zone appears to have "lesser chances of success in the eighties in comparison to the previous decade".[11]

To accelerate the process of international peace, "measures of arms control and disarmament as well as political measures" have to be strengthened. The concept of Peace Zone in this context should be understood not as a policy but as a mission, a movement, irrespective of the mounting tensions and increasing political instabilities. Efforts for the realization of this concept in one form or the other must continue in the interest of security of mankind.

REFERENCES

1. *SIPRI Year Book*. 1972, p. 557.
2. *Ibid.*, p. 551.
3. W.A.C. Adie, *Oil Politics and Sea Power: Indian Ocean*, 1975, p. 1.
4. Ceylon's Memorandum on Indian Ocean Security.
5. C.W. Raymond, "East Africa and the Indian Ocean : A Zone of Peace", *African Affairs*, July, 1977, p. 339.
6. K.R. Singh, *Indian Ocean : Big Power Presence and Local Response*, 1977, p. 225.
7. Howaed Wriggins, "The Indian Ocean : Five Years Later", A Paper presented at a Conference on Indian Ocean, University of California, Berkely, May, 1976.
8. Denneth Bonlding, *Stable Peace*, London, 1978, p. 64.
9. Hedlay Bull, *The Control of Arms Race*, London, 1961, p. 75.
10. *India in the World Strategic Environment,* The Institute for Defence Studies and Analyses, New Delhi, 1973, p. 716.
11. K.S. Sidhu, "Indian Ocean as a Zone of Peace" *The Economic Times*, Bombay, 23 November, 1980.

CHAPTER VI

Emerging Issues

Indian Ocean in Global Strategies : Some Perspectives

The Indian Ocean plays a significant role in strategic and space war scenarios. It is interesting to note the broad parallelism in the chronology of the development of direct ascent HIT system against the background of US strategies and military deployment in the Indian Ocean :

1962	:	Investigation initiated for HIT by USAF Space Systems Division. The US Navy Pacific Fleet started visit to Indian Ocean.
1965-66	:	Diego-Garcia created as British Indian Ocean Territory, believed to have been done on US initiatives. Diego Garcia leased to the US for defence purposes after local population transferred to Mauritius.
1969	:	USAF explored direct ascent ASAT (anti-satellite) report.
1970	:	Diego Garcia communication stations became operational.
1975	:	USAF proposed miniature space interceptor.
1976	:	Anglo-US agreement to expand the scope and role of Diego Garcia.
1977	:	USAF approved $ 58.7 million contract for ground launched, direct ascent, non-nuclear ASAT. Concept of RDF created. Large-scale joint naval-air exercise including Mindlink-77

in which the US (with aircraft carriers Enterprise and Midway), the UK, Iran and Pakistan took part in NW Indian Ocean.

1980-83 : Diego Garcia expanded as naval-air base. The US naval carrier task force deployed in Indian Ocean, level increased to two carrier battle groups in 1983.

1984-90 : ASANT Missile with MHV (miniature homing vehicle) weapon based on HIT test fired from F-15 on January 21, 1984 in space. Initial operational capability planned for 1987 with 28 weapons with one F-15 squadron. Employment of MHV weapon on European Tornado ADV planned. Diego Garcia expansion facilities completed. Masirah/Oman build-up planned for completion besides other facilities in the Indian Ocean.

The Soviet strategy in the Indian Ocean region is guided, in a large measure, by parameters and objectives similar to that of the United States, and may also be seen to operate in bi-planar dimensions. Perhaps the strongest incentives flow from the desire to secure a role for the Soviet navy to support the status of the Soviet Union as a global, 'super' power.

As a country with a Super Power status, its motives to extend its influence, especially in the Third World, are as high as that of the United States. The Indian Ocean and its littoral area of even greater interest to the Soviet Union because of their geographic proximity with each other. In more ways than one, the Indian Ocean and its littoral constitute the soft, vulnerable underbelly of the Soviet Union in strategic terms. Any US moves in this region, inevitably, must be seen by the Soviet Union as hostile and a threat to the Soviet security. The 'choke points' of Suez Canal-Horn of Africa and the Malacca Straits region and the larger 'gateways' to Indian Ocean dominated by pro-US countries like Australia and South Africa place severe limitations on the Soviet ability to extend influence in the Indian Ocean. They also impose an even greater strategic limitations to its ability to redeploy and reinforce its naval capabilities in the Pacific and the Atlantic Oceans. Given the markedly lower level of naval power of the Soviet Union as compared to that of the US and its allies, the Soviet deployable naval power in the Indian Ocean is very limited. The Western strategists view the enhanced U.S. naval air deployment in the Indian Ocean as a means to force the Soviet Union to further fragmentate and split its naval power providing increased opportunities for the US and its allies to achieve favourable concentration of forces in time and space. Thus, in the foreseeable future, the Soviet naval power in the Indian Ocean may be expected to continue following a reactive strategy, with a comparatively low level of forces deployment. This level is inadequate to directly challenge the US naval air power, an adequate visible index of the Soviet power in the Third World.

As regards deployment of the Soviet military power as an instrument of policy, a study carried out by the US Brookings Institution lists a total of 167 instances of the Soviet deployment of force without war between 1946-79 (US deployment of forces for the same period comes to 231 instances). Out of these, 27 incidents (16.1%) affected the Indian Ocean and its littoral. The average number of incidents of Soviet use of force without war in the Indian ocean region for this period works out to 0.82 per year (compared to an average of 1.33 per year in the case of the United States). Thus a degree of parallelism between the Super Powers' global strategies as operative in the Indian Ocean is in evidence vis-a-vis the Third World countries of the Indian Ocean region. The Soviet limitation is the outcome of its handicap in strategic mobility and naval-air power projection capabilities as compared to the US.

The Soviet naval presence in the Indian Ocean can hardly be construed as a challenge or even as a result of 'rivalry with the United States'. As a matter of fact, the Soviet naval forces in the Indian Ocean have very limited offensive capabilities outmatched even by Pakistan. Reinforcements from the Pacific/North Atlantic fleets would take upwards of 18-30 days. This modest naval presence may be seen to be motivated more by a strategy of creating a foothold in the Indian Ocean, showing the flag and support to friendly nations.

Global Interdependence

A great deal of the arguments in relation to the geopolitical and Super Power rivalry in the Indian Ocean revolve around the subject of natural (especially scarce) resources. The Soviet threat to the Western access to these resources forms the basis of the Western policy formulations with regard to the Indian Ocean region. Gulf oil is the most important resource essential to the West. In fact it is cited as the immediate reason for the presence of two carrier battle groups of the US Navy and warships of the other Western countries in the Arabian Sea. It also forms the basic justification for the creation of the US Cent Com and the proliferating RDFs. Two points relating to some Gulf oil myths merit notice in this regard. The USSR is not dependent on the energy and mineral resources of the Indian Ocean littoral. At the same time, interdication of the Western shipping and denial of the Western access to essential energy and mineral resources could hardly be considered seriously as a policy option because of the limited pay offs and the very high levels of risk involved. Secondly, it is also not very certain whether the West really believes in its own professed theories in this regard. To cite an example, the threat of possible closure of the Straits of Hormuz has received intense international attention, especially since the beginning of Iran - Iraq war in September 1980. Large forces have been positioned in the vicinity to keep the Straits 'open'; and investments in arms supplies and security arrangement have been made in the region leading to expenditure of billions of dollars. An alternative to the 'vulnerability' of the Hormuz 'choke-point' could have been the construction of a pipe line, by-passing the choke point and leading directly to the Arabian Sea. The countries concerned are already part of the Gulf Cooperation Council. Extending a pipe line from Kuwait to Masirah/Oman (a distance of about 1,000 miles) may well be in the order of $ 200 million, a figure representing possibly one week's cost of maintaining the naval armada near the Straits of Hormuz. At the same time, the only pipeline constructed in this period has been to Yanbu in the Red Sea half-way between the two 'choke points' of Suez Canal and the Horn of Africa.

The fact is that the politico-economic links of the world are interwoven in a complex mesh of global interdependence. The United States is not only inextricably involved in foreign markets for raw materials, but also imports substantial amount of manufactured goods and even technology. Similarly, other nations depend upon the United States as a market for their products and as a source of technology goods and services to support their economies.

While the US economy still greatly influences the world economic system, many other nations and coalitions of nations are assuming important roles. This growing politico-economic interdependence has created for the West what is perceived as a global challenge. This interdependence has also made the industrialised nations (Western and Eastern) more susceptible to the increasing independence and strength of the Third World countries. This is viewed as an additional challenge in a 'North-South' conflict, portrayed as Third World trade unionism. To retain a favourable position in the trade structure of the world and global politico-economic interdependence, the industrialised developed countries seek to control and influence these structures and interdependence to their own advantage. Many options have been and are being formulated towards these objectives ranging from substitution of economic aid by arms supplies on controlled terms and selective basis. Coercive diplomacy, politics of intrusion, deployment military force, proliferation of Rapid Deployment Force and increasing militarisation of the Indian Ocean are manifestations of this quest for control and influence. In this scenario, the inherent instability of the underdeveloped countries of the Indian Ocean region seeking to establish themselves as nation-States, the large number of micro-States with their vulnerability to external pressure and regional conflicts and rivalries tend to work to the advantage of the strategies and interests of the devleoped industrialised world represented by the two Super Powers and their allies.

The Ocean of the non-aligned and developing countries is almost landlocked in the north and does not extend into the cold regions towards the south. Its northern entry points are controlled by narrow waters, and the two Super Powers are furthest from its southern waters. Its physical configuration is such that it provides certain choke-points of control : whichever power controls the Suez Canal, the Malacca Straits, the Cape of Good Hope and the Australian waters can exercise significant control over the Indian Ocean region. Among the 47 littoral and hinterland countries, only South Africa, Australia and Israel and developed and, excepting these three and Thailand, the rest are non-aligned. Half of the States of this region have less than 5 million population. Out of more than 1200 million inhabitants in the region, 72% live in the Indian sub-continent (and of these almost three-fifths in India).[1] Significantly, some of the less populated countries, like Saudi Arabia and Zambia, possess some of the most important and strategic natural resources which are needed for the economic sustenance of the world in general and of the OECD countries in particular.

The scramble for the natural resources of the Indian Ocean has added to its strategic importance. More than 65 per cent of world's uranium and known oil reserves are in this area, and some 40 per cent of world's off-shore oil production comes from the Indian Ocean Coastal States. Besides the Persian Gulf, areas of off shore oil supplies are the continental shelves around the Indian sub-continent, off North-West Australia, near Mauritius and around South Africa, large deposits of manganese containing iron, copper, nickel and cobalt have been found in the eastern part of the Indian Ocean (within and outside 200 mile zone), and near Mauritius and Madagascar (at depths of between 3500 and 5000 metres). In the Red Sea at depths of about 200 metres, deposits on the sea-bed are of zinc, copper, lead, silver, vandadium and molybedenum. It may be noted that presently India is the only Third World country with the capacity for sea-bed exploration : (In 1981, an Indian exploration ship obtained manganese nodules from a depth of 4500 metres in Indian's south-west economic zone).[2] It is estimated that in 1985, out of the 27 million barrel per day required by the OECD countries, 15.3 mbd (or 56 per cent) of the oil would have to come from the Persian Gulf.

Besides the natural resources, the Indian Ocean waterlanes provide main transport connections vital for the trade and economy of the West. Every year, around 30,000 ships (including 1500 oil-tankers) travel the sea routes of the Indian Ocean through the Suez Canal, Bal-el-Mandeb Straits, Malacca Straits, Hormuz Straits, around the Cape of Good Hope and through the Mozambique-Madagascar Channel. In the mid-seventies, whereas the regional trade was only 18%,the Indian Ocean States' total trade with the OECD countries was 65 per cent. Apart from oil, there are other products of the area which are vital for world trade and the dependence of the West on these products is considerable.

Once this dependence was created, it was safe to encourage local conflicts with the surity that the war-affected economies would seek help to rebuild their economic structure and replenish arms supplies and that the oil supplies would not be affected because the Gulf economies' dependence on oil for revenue is total. The second objective of the OECD strategy, namely, non-intervention of the third party in the Gulf, is more difficult to achieve, and the threat is all too real. The geostrategic conditions for a pre-emptive Soviet action are favourable and the West has limited means for averting/deterring such a move.[3]

The Soviet Union is also trying to secure a 'Zone of Soviet penetration' in this region by exploiting the regional instability and a general resentment against the West. A distance of only 1100 km. separates the Baku area of the USSR from Abadan and Basra. The Soviet Union concentrates one of its strongest air-contingents in this area.[4] The Soviet Union is slowly altering the military balance of forces to her own advantage: "The Soviet Union is making increasing use of its strategic position and is leaving it to the other side to make itself politically vulnerable through its endeavours to obtain facilities in the Indian Ocean area".[5]

In the Indian Ocean area, the Soviet interests are governed not only by political-economic considerations but also by strategic facts. The Indian Ocean assumed strategic significance for the Soviet Union after the development of nuclear-powered submarines capable of launching nuclear medium-range ballistic missiles. The physical configuration of the Indian Ocean is such that from here strategic weapon deployment can be made against the Soviet Union, but it cannot be so used against the US which is altogether in a different hemisphere.

If the Soviet Union has to neutralise these new weapon systems or if she has to present a similar threat to the West, control of the Indian Ocean is necessary. The Soviet naval strategy, therefore, shifted from sea-denial to sea-control. Therefore, the Indian Ocean became vital for the Soviet Union as it forms an all-weather transit route for transfer of fleet units between the Soviet Far Eastern and Black Sea fleets, Baltic and Northern fleets.

The United States has clear strategic interests and objectives in the Indian Ocean: "The US has both a conventional and perhaps a strategic nuclear military interest in the Indian Ocean. Military objectives for US conventional forces include the capability to (i) protect US economic interests in the Persian Gulf, (ii) employ or threaten to use force in support of US diplomatic objectives in the Middle East, (iii) secure the Indian Ocean air and sea routes against harassment or interdiction, (iv) intervene in support of other objectives in the littoral and related to all of these, (v) balance Soviet Forces in the region and attain superiority in a crisis. The US also possesses a potential strategic nuclear military objectives of deploying, when necessary or convenient ballistic missiles submarines targeted on the USSR".[6] The US vital interests include the preservation of the Western access to the Persian Gulf oil resources, and the maintenance of a local geopolitical balance. The US believes that any decisive threat to these interests can originate only from the Soviet action in the region or from such action interwoven with intra-regional instability. This challenge to the US position is not just theoretical but very much real, as was evidenced by the Soviet action in Afghanistan and the Horn of Africa.

This coercive diplomacy in the Indian Ocean region is based on clear policy objectives. The US believes that demonstrative uses of armed force can be an effective way of securing its objectives. The search for bases in the Indian Ocean, the establishment of the RDF (Rapid Deployment Force), and the massive consolidation of facilities at Diego Garcia are all geared towards the use of coercive diplomacy. The objective is to ensure the sustained flow of oil to the industrialised Western countries. It is an open secret that the real target of the RDF is Saudi Arabian-Berri oilfield; off shore oilfields of Abqaiq, Damman, Chawar and Qatif; the complexes of Juaymeh and Ras Tanura; Damman Port; Dharan air-base; Hormuz Straits and the capital Riyadh — which can be swiftly captured in the face of any Soviet threat. The RDF, as an 'over-the-horizon' capability, provides protection to the legitimacy of the Saudi monarchy against any internal upheavals.

The United States has emphasized that the reason for maintaining a permanent presence in the Indian Ocean may change from time to time, but the objective would not. First, the reason was to secure uninterrupted oil supply and then it was to counter the threat from the Soviet action in Afghanistan. But the objective remains the maintenance of regional balance of power and to prevent any adverse shifts. It is for this reason that a US naval presence in the Indian Ocean is highly advantageous. The US submarines operating in the Indian Ocean can cover many significant Soviet and Chinese targets from there, but the Soviet submarines operating in the area cannot reach any part of the USA. Therefore from the strategic point of view, a presence in the Indian Ocean is of utmost importance for the United States.

The Area and Its Significance

The Indian Ocean area—comprising the third largest body of waters and its littoral and hinterland — is vast and is of crucial significance when we consider the water space it covers and the countries and the populations it includes. The real and potential resources it is known to possess, the important transit routes of trade and commerce it offers, and the political and military strategy it calls for, has aroused unprecedented interest among world leaders as well as academics who are exploring and researching the various facets of the area. That the developments in the area have engaged the attention of some of the most important organs of the United Nations since 1971 is a further indication of its significance.

The Indian Ocean is over 6,500 miles in length (north to south) and nearly 6,000 miles in breadth (east to west). It covers nearly 20.6 per cent of the total oceanic area of the world. Its area and the distances are thus enormous. The Bay of Bengal alone covers an area equal to half of Europe. It is 13,000 feet deep which makes it deeper than the Atlantic. It unique feature is that it is a more or less landlocked ocean having a land roof, a situation which is found neither in the Atlantic nor in the Pacific.

The precise delineation of the Indian Ocean has been a subject of discussion both within and outside the United Nations. It is suggested that the dividing line between the Indian

Ocean and the Atlantic Ocean should be the Meridian of Cape Agulhas (20.0' E); the dividing line between it and the Pacific should be the Meridian of the Southest Cape of Tasmania (147.0' E), the western exit of the Bass Strait and the median line between north-west Australia and the peninsula of Malay (the Cape of Sumatra). As for it southern limits, it is suggested that 60°S should divide it from the Antarctic. If these boundaries of the Indian Ocean are agreed upon, its area would be approximately 75 million square miles.

Power Vacuum and the Presence of Outside Powers

Sea power and power on land are inextricably interwoven in practically all situations. The Indian Ocean area is no exception to the general rule. This is confirmed by the events since ancient times. For instance, activities in the Indian Ocean were dramatically increased and continued for many centuries after the consolidation of the empire of the Mauryas in India leading to substantial political, cultural, and commercial contacts between India and many States of Asia and Europe.

A study of the history of sea power in the Indian Ocean would show that on account of its enormous size, it was not possible for any power till a couple of centuries ago to exercise any decisive influence. Different countries dominated different sectors or parts of the Ocean. Modern history of the Ocean begins with the voyage of Vasco da Gama in 1494, at a time when neither any littoral nor outside power was of any consequence in the Ocean. The Portuguese had a shrewd sense of politics and strategy and therefore they gave attention to both the major sectors — east and west — of this vast expanse of water. In spite of this, they could not hold on for more than about a century. The Dutch entered the scene in the late sixteenth and the early seventeenth centuries. The French and the British initiated their efforts and competition in the following decade of the seventeenth century.

Without going into the power struggle in the Indian Ocean in detail between the European powers in the eighteenth and the early nineteenth centuries, we may note here that under the peace arrangements made in 1815 at the Congress of Vienna, Britain's sway over the Indian Ocean became more or less complete, a situation which continued for a century and a half.

This is not to say that under Pax Britannia things were always smooth. With the opening of the Suez Canal in 1869, a project accomplished by the French without British participation, the element of competition and rivalry increased, and consequently the British dominance over the Ocean was impaired.

The Indian Ocean obviously could not escape the logic of the political changes that were taking place in its coastal areas. These changes also profoundly affected the British position as a Power in international relations of the post-war period, not only in political terms but in economic and other related fields as well. The British land and air forces had to be either completely withdrawn from most of these coastal areas of the Ocean or substantially reduced. There was some diminution in the naval strength also. In spite of these developments, the British naval power was a decisive military factor — particularly in Southeast Asia—in the balance of power in the Indian Ocean. The British persisted in maintaining this posture ostensibly on the ground that it would protect their economic interests in the area.

To start with, it may be argued that the theory of power vacuum was based on an assessment of dubious validity as regards the importance of Britain to an area which had been politically transformed in a fundamental manner. Instead of being pockets and parcels belonging to Imperial Powers, the area now had multiple polities which were sovereign, self-respecting members of the community of nations and which brooked no interference by outside Powers. In the changed situation the British role was inconsequential. Even if Britain had not wanted to withdraw, it would not have been possible for it to play any major role in the area. An army of 70,000 men, supported by a small air and naval power, could not play any significant role in such a huge area. A few instances are sufficient to substantiate this point. More than once the British troops did suppress violence in Mauritius which was by no means a major military operation, but when it came to bigger situations Britain was more or less helpless. But it could do precious little when violent eruptions occurred in Aden, or when conflicts between India and Pakistan broke out. Thus, it is clear that once the British possessions attained their political freedom, such military strength as it continued to retain in some parts of the Ocean, became a matter of marginal significance from politico-strategic standpoint. Any talk, therefore, about the emergence of a power vacuum in this area as a consequence of the total withdrawal of the British is against the realities of the situation.

Rooted in the traditional theory of balance of power, the power vacuum concept suggests that the new nations of Asia and Africa in the Indian Ocean are economically so poor and politically so vulnerable as to be unable to defend themselves from within as well as from without. A typical Western view representing the above position is to be found, for instance, in an editorial of *The New York Times* which said:

> The harsh reality is that a complete British withdrawal.....would leave dangerous power vacuum over a vast and volatile area which the United States' and Britain's other allies would find it extremely difficult to fill, a vacuum that would serve neither Britain's long term interests nor its stakes in world peace and stability.[7]

In the context of the rivalry between the Super Powers, this line of thinking has certain implications.

First, if, taking advantage of the weak and inadequately defended area, one of the two Super Powers were not to act, it would lag behind the other. The other Power would then take advantage of the situation and initiate the necessary moves to promote its interests in the area and thus create an unfavourable balance of power situation.

Second, the littoral countries need some sort of a guar-dian or caretaker in the area to protect them from possible mischief from the influence-seeking outside Powers. This is supposed to be in the interest of the countries in the region because, if left unprotected, they would succumb to the pressures of outside Powers equipped with far superior economic and military might.

Third, the conflict situation in certain parts of the littoral provides a tempting pasture for the outside Powers, particularly those which feel that their interests and obligations extend to this area. This is so because the littoral is conflict-prone. In the southern part of Africa, for instance, there have been clashes between the small number of whites who hold crucial positions and the overwhelming number of blacks. In West Asia there has been a continued armed confrontation between Israel and the Arabs and a situation of 'no war, no peace' still persists. In South Asia there have been conflicts between India and Pakistan, which, though local, were among the most serious of the kind. In Southeast Asia apart from Vietnam, several conflicts have occurred and more may recur in future. In all these conflicts the Super Powers have been present by proxy. Their resources—economic and military—have played a vital role in sharpening these conflicts. According to the power vacuum theory, if one Super Power is attempting to influence the course of events in a conflict, the other Super Power should also enter the race by aiding and supporting the other party in the conflict, so that a disadvantageous balance-of-power situation may not be created for itself.

Finally, in international relations, it is well-known how the Super Powers have at times endeavoured either to support regimes which, whether or not representative or legitimate, are convenient to them, or to subvert regimes which are inconvenient to them. A very interesting feature of this subterranean activity is that these Powers have always disclaimed it. Hence, though it is not clearly and openly articulated, implicit in the power vacuum concept is the desire of the outside Powers to influence the domestic situation in littoral countries if it turns out to be unfavourable to them and if the cost does not outweigh the benefits.

The Soviets have, at least in theory, denounced the concept of a power vacuum without any reservation and characterized it as a 'notorious thesis'. A Soviet commentator wrote in Izvestia that "a vacuum is an airless void, a term quite inappropriate when speaking of our planet today. Hardly any political 'blank spots', by which I mean places without independent states, are left".[8] Thus, the Soviet Union appears to be in sympathy with littoaral sentiment that the idea of a power vacuum smacks of imperialist thinking.

The Sea Power Concept

A power which dominates the sea has decisive advantages over its rivals. It can control the maritime trade, which is becoming more and more important. It can easily transport its army to fight in any area and thus dominate even the littoral, because the means of communication over the high sea even today are much superior to, and faster than, those available overland. It can use its navy for blockade, for shore bombardment and for landing troops and materials at a given point and time, and thus threaten its rivals. If pressed, it can even retreat into the high seas and be sure that its forces will not be totally annihilated. These advantages which are valid even today, when sea power has to compete with air power, were even more valuable two centuries ago.

Several theories were propounded on the need to dominate the oceans. One of the first persons who popularized the concept of sea power was Alfred Thayer Mahan (1840-1914). He wrote several books to highlight the need to control the high seas.[9] There is no doubt that Mahan's theory had a great influence upon the evolution of naval strategy. Even today his basic presumptions are valid, despite the fact that the navy has to face a serious challenge from the air force and from the missile system. Control of the waves, and the waters beneath them, is all the more important today in the context of sophisticated weapons system like the nuclear-power submarine capable of launching a medium or long-range ballistic or cruise missile even when submerged. This new weapons systems, in combination with the traditional vessels, gives the navy a big power not only to command the seas, but also increase the range of its armament from the high seas to any place on the earth. Thus, the navy can truly play strategic role which is 'global' in the real sense.

Thus, the control of the littoral became important to ensure a trouble-free functioning of the new weapons system which was being deployed in the Indian Ocean. The confrontation between the Super Powers on the land and in the sea also involved them in regional politics. The resultant fall-out of the Cold War affected the littoral states in the Indian Ocean area as well. The policy of non-alignment, which sought a way out of that dilemma, failed to win support from many of the littoral states. The USA, in its bid to win over local powers, pumped economic and military aid in the areas of its influence. The Soviet Union also developed friendly ties with several states in the area.

Thus, the Indian Ocean area, which was free from the Super Power rivalry in the first half of the 1950s, was subsequently dominated by it. Regional tensions are linked with the Super Power rivalry in the area, which is influenced by the weapon systems and strategy based upon them. Crisis-management has become increasingly difficult, since the area has grown more and more important for the Super Power and the big powers in their future global strategy.

The change-over, from land-based to ocean-based strategy, brought about a detente on land, especially in Europe, and to some extent in Asia. But whereas the European detente might be more lasting, the detente in Asia has proved to be illusory. Europe is getting united and is strong, economically and militarily, to pose as a third force. The Indian Ocean littoral is weak and divided. Thanks to the new weapons system, the Super Powers confrontation has moved from land to sea, an area with no clear territorial demarcation, and, therefore, is likely to pose more problems to those who are situated on its littoral. The Indian Ocean area thus becomes involved in the Super Power confrontation, based upon a weapon system which ipso facto demands control of the high seas for its effective utilization. The confrontation, which started after the system was perfected, will continue unless the littoral states suceed in making the Indian Ocean area a Peace Zone.

The Desire for a Peace Zone

The reaction of the Indian Ocean states to the growing Super Power rivalry in the area, right from the 1960s, was in keeping with their traditional policies. Those countries which were aligned to either of the Super Powers, or had treaty relations with any of the big powers, were in favour of the continuation of the old alliances. Some of them began to strengthen their relations with the Western Powers. Thus, Australia came closer to the USA. South Africa began to develop close relations with France and West Germany which were not only trying to develop roots but were also striving to replace Great Britain as the dominant power in that region.

While these White regimes in the Indian Ocean came closer to the Western powers, the attitude of erstwhile 'committed'

Afro-Asian states underwent a significant change. The gradual military disengagement of the West, and the parallel Soviet drive to win more friends, brought about a marked change in the attitude of these states. Though some of them continued to be members of the SEATO and the CENTO, or to honour their commitments under the mutual security agreements, they began to follow a more independent foreign policy. The Cold War rivalry, and the consequent political and military fall-out in the Third World, was opposed as being detrimental not only to world peace but also to local security and unity. The SEATO and the Baghdad Pact were opposed by the non-aligned states, not only because they brought the Cold War to a relatively low-tension area, but also because the massive military support by one bloc to a few countries in the Third World would intensify regional disputes. They also felt that military imbalance, created by the massive military aid to a few countries would trigger-off an arms race which would divert the scarce financial resources towards acquiring and maintaining armed forces out of all proportion to their national resources. This would, in turn, seriously jeopardize their economic development programmes.

The entry of the US task force in 1964 in the region was a continuation of the Super Power confrontation, and the non-aligned countries reacted to it as they had reacted to similar situations earlier. For them, it was a continuation of the old Cold War confrontation. They realized that the American naval presence in the Indian Ocean would invite the Soviet presence, and the Cold War rivalry would be carried to the high seas, where the littoral countries would have even less chances of influencing it. The non-aligned countries began demanding, as early as 1964, that the big power presence should be removed from the Indian Ocean.

Mrs. Bandaranaike, the then Prime Minister of Sri Lanka, took lead in the matter. In her speech on 8 October, 1964 at the Second Non-aligned Nations Conference at Cairo, she forcefully argued that the concept of a nuclear-free zone should be applied to the oceans also, especially to oceans like the Indian Ocean and the South Atlantic which had remained free from nuclear weapons till then. She also said that Sri Lanka had closed its sea-ports and airfields to ships and aircrafts which either carried nuclear weapons or were equipped for nuclear warfare. She recommended that other non-aligned countries should also follow that principle. Mrs. Bandaranaike's suggestions were subsequently incorporated in the declaration of the Cairo Conference, which is also known as the Programme for Peace and International Cooperation. Part VII of that programme dealt with disarmament, denuclearization and the establishment of nuclear-free zones. Part VIII condemned the expressed intention of the big powers to establish bases in the Indian Ocean as a 'calculated attempt to intimidate the emerging countries of Africa and Asia and an unwarranted extension of the policy of neo-colonialism and imperialism'. The question was also debated at the Non-aligned Nations Conference at Algiers, and a resolution reiterating support for a Peace-Zone in the Indian Ocean was passed.

In keeping with their earlier stand, the non-aligned countries took strong exception to the plan to construct Anglo-American bases in the Indian Ocean islands, especially in Diego Garcia. Dinesh Singh, the then Deputy Minister for External Affairs, said, as early as 18 November, 1965, that the Indian government strongly opposed the construction of any foreign base in the Indian Ocean. He said that India would do everything possible to resist the establishment of an Anglo-American base in the Chagos archipelago. Several other States in the Indian Ocean area were also critical of such arrangements. The British and the American Governments tried to pacify the Indian Ocean States by assuring that the proposed base at Diego Garcia not be a naval or air base but only a communication base. Hardly anyone was taken in by their explanations. Another interesting argument used to justify the increasing Western presence in the Indian Ocean area, as mentioned earlier was based upon the so-called 'vacuum' theory. The argument gained some weight because of the dramatic entry of a small Soviet naval task force in the Indian Ocean in 1968, which coincided with the British decision of partial withdrawal from the area.

The two moves were parallel but not interconnected. The growing American nuclear presence in the Indian Ocean was threatening the southern flank of the Soviet Union, which was exposed to any attack launched from there by the Polaris submarines. The Soviet Union was concerned with it, especially after the closure of the Suez Canal since June 1967. It effectively blocked the direct line of communication from the Black Sea and the Mediterranean Sea to the Indian Ocean and prevented the Soviet Union from putting enough naval force to counter the growing American presence in the Indian Ocean. The Soviet Union would have attempted to counter that threat even if Britain had decided not to withdraw from the area. Gradual withdrawal by Britain from the area was due to its shrinking economic and military capacity and the growing local opposition to its presence in the area. Britain maintained its presence, though a reduced one, in Southeast Asia, the Persian Gulf and in the British territories in the Indian Ocean. It entered into an alliance with the U.S.A. to operate jointly in the Indian Ocean by strengthening their presence in the islands which were controlled by Britain. Thus, the supporters of the vacuum theory were wrongly correlating two parallel events, while justifying the increased American presence in the area.

The Indian government, as also others, strongly objected to the so-called vacuum theory. Mrs. Gandhi emphasized that point during her tour of the Southeast Asian countries in May 1966. In her Press Conferences in Singapore, Canberra, Wellington and Kuala Lumpur, she repeatedly emphasized the fact that the withdrawal of the British forces from the area would not create any vacuum, and, if any vacuum was created, it ought to be filled by the local powers themselves and not by outside powers. She pointed out that the entry of outside forces would not only create more tensions but also accentuate those which already prevailed in the area. In her press conference in Singapore, she rejected the idea that India should fill the gap left by the British. Baliram Bhagat, Minister of State in the Ministry of External Affairs, elaborated the point further in the debate in the Rajya Sabha on 25 July, 1968. He said, 'We believe that the security of the countries in the region must rest ultimately on their own national strength, and on their willing cooperation between one another as sovereign independent states'. This fact was reiterated in the joint communiques issued after Mrs. Gandhi's visit to Singapore, on 20 May 1968, and after the visit of Dr. Ramgoolam, the Prime Minister of Mauritius, to India on 16 December, 1969. The Non-aligned Nations Summit Conference at Lusaka, in September 1970, also discussed the question. The declaration adopted by the Conference, inter alia, called upon all states:

> to consider and respect the Indian Ocean as a Zone of Peace from which great power rivalries and competition as well as bases conceived in the context of such rivalries and competition—either army, navy or air force bases —are excluded. The area should also be free of nuclear weapons.

International support for the idea of converting the Indian Ocean into a Peace Zone got a greater boost after 1972. The joint communique, issued on 6 June, 1973, following the visit of Whitlam, the Prime Minister of Australia, to India, urged for the creation of a Zone of Peace in the Indian Ocean and said that it would be a positive step towards the reduction of tensions and rivalries in the area. In a joint declaration on 30 November 1973, Mrs. Gandhi and Brezhnev reaffirmed their readiness to participate, together with other states concerned, on an equal basis, in finding a fair solution to the question of making the Indian Ocean a Zone of Peace. The Prime Minister of the Maldives, while visiting India in March 1974, expressed his full support to the concept of the Indian Ocean as a Zone of Peace, free from great power rivalries, tension and military escalation. The concept was also reiterated during Mrs. Gandhi's Iran visit in May 1974.

The Indian Ocean Question before the United Nations

The matter of the Indian Ocean being free from big power and super power rivalry had been agitating the minds of the Afro-Asian leaders since the switchover from the I.C.B.M. to the S.L.B.M. weapons system as the main force behind the strategic-nuclear deterrence. The question was debated in various Afro-Asian and non-aligned conferences. In September 1971, fifty-four members of the non-aligned group met at the U.N. and decided on concrete steps that should be taken to implement the Lusaka Declaration, relating to the creation of a Peace Zone in the Indian Ocean.[10] The delegate of Sri Lanka, Hamilton Shirley Amerasinghe, requested the Secretary General on 1 October 1971, for the inclusion of the item in the agenda of the twentyeighth session. Tanzania joined at as a co-sponsor on 7 October.

If one analyzes the question of creating a Peace Zone in the Indian Ocean, and the discussion on that question both within and outside the United Nations, one come to the following conclusion. The U.N. resolutions have gained sufficient majority in the General Assembly but most of the great powers and major maritime powers have abstained from voting on the resolution and have shown a marked reluctance to attend the conference on the Indian Ocean. Thus, despite the overwhelming majority in the General Assembly, the resolution is, in fact, ineffective. Secondly, there are marked differences even among the Indian Ocean states on the ways and means to establish a Peace Zone in the area. Some states have already introduced new elements which have no direct bearing upon the basic question of elimination of the foreign presence conceived in the context of great power rivalry from the Indian Ocean. In 1974 and 1975, the question of creating a nuclear-weapon-free zone in South Asia was projected as a major issue which overshadowed the question of creating a Peace Zone in the Indian Ocean. New ideas about forms of political regime and regional arms limitation were also projected as a precondition to the creation of a Peace Zone in the area. The idea of a mutual balance between the great powers as the best way of preserving peace in the area was also mooted. Undoubtedly, such diversionary tactics not only detract the attention from the main issue, but also enable the interested foreign powers to pursue their policy of divide and rule and ultimately scuttle the major issue—the elimination of great-power presence from the Indian Ocean.

The Future of the Peace Zone Idea

There is no denying the fact that the great-power presence in the Indian Ocean has increased tremendously since 1964, when the idea of a Peace Zone was first mooted by the Afro-Asian states. The U.S.A. has not only constructed its military base in Diego Garcia but has also expanded the facilities there to enhance its strategic-nuclear as well as conventional interventionist capabilities. The visits of the U.S. task force have also increased since the October War. The French too have strengthened their presence in the Island of Reunion and in Djibouti. There are reports that the Soviet Union also is keen to match the Western presence in the area. The Chairman of the U.N. Ad Hoc

Committee on the Indian Ocean, H.S. Amerasinghe, drew attention to the U.S. strategic-nuclear presence in the Indian Ocean in his statement at an informal meeting of the littoral and hinterland states of the Indian Ocean, in New York, on 16 April 1973.[11] He also pointed out that the U.S.A. seemed to enjoy a greater advantage as their submarines in the Indian Ocean could cover many important Soviet and Chinese targets. He added that the Soviet submarines, on the other hand, could not reach any part of the United States with their missiles from the Indian Ocean, and that they were not necessary for action against the Chinese targets. He concluded : 'It would appear, therefore, that the initiative in removing a strategic nuclear role in the Indian Ocean rests primarily on the United States and that such a step would not endanger its security'.

The U.S.A. has, however, not shown any inclination to remove its nuclear presence from this area. The U.S. ambassador to India, Daniel P. Moynihan, told the newsmen in Madras on 4 March 1974 that Diego Garcia was 1,600 kilometres away from India and there was nothing of fundamental concern for Indians there. He said that the global strategy of the U.S.A. and its fundamental interests required a base on that island notwithstanding what friendly countries might feel about it. He even questioned the very name of the Indian Ocean, 'Why call it the Indian Ocean? One may well call it the Madagascar Sea', he said.[12]

Swaran Singh, while commenting upon the remarks of Moynihan said in the Lok Sabha, on 6 March 1974, 'Who is he to change the name of the Indian Ocean? It is a fact of geography and not a gift of the U.S. Government or its ambassador'.

The opposition to the great-power presence in the Indian Ocean is steadily growing. If one looks at the voting pattern in the U.N. on the General Assembly's resolutions on the Indian Ocean, one finds that gradually more and more states have started voting for the resolution. In December 1971, only sixty-one countries voted for the resolution and fifty-five abstained from voting. Among them there were several littoral states like Australia, Madagascar, New Zealand, South Yemen, Singapore, South Africa and Thailand. In 1972, the number of members voting for the resolution increased to ninety-five, only thirty-five abstained. Oman, South Africa and Thailand were the only littoral states that abstained. In 1974, the number of members voting for the resolution increased to one hundred and four, and only twenty-six abstained. There was no abstention from among the littoral states. Thus, one can see that by 1974 all the littoral and hinterland states had voted for the resolution declaring the Indian Ocean as a Peace Zone.

Despite this growing support for the concept of a Peace Zone in the Indian Ocean, two facts must be noted. The first is that the voting pattern shows that most of the great powers, which have a presence in the Indian Ocean, continued to abstain on the resolution. Also, they refused to enter into consultation with the Ad Hoc Committee of the U.N. which had been entrusted the task of finding ways and means of implementing the General Assembly resolutions. Second, all these resolutions talk about the need to create a Peace Zone in the context of Great Power rivalry. This undue emphasis in the U.N. resolutions upon great power rivalry is unfortunate and poses constraints. It strengthens the arguments of those powers in favour of maintaining their presence in the area. They argue that they are there because others are also there. Secondly, it automatically gives credibility to the arguments of those who are advocating a balanced force in the area. It also totally ignores the fact that peace in a given region can be disturbed by a Great Power presence in the area on issues which may not be linked even remotely with the Great Power rivalry. It overlooks the growing conventional-interventionist presence of some great powers in the Indian Ocean. Therefore, serious attention should be given to delinking the question of creating a Peace Zone in the Indian Ocean, from the Great Power rivalry in the area so that the question of removing the presence of each foreign power should be studied separately.

Besides taking concerted action in the United Nations, the littoral states are also devising means to limit the foreign presence in the area. Three options have been suggested so far; creating regional nuclear-weapon-free zones, neutralization of the region, and the balanced force idea. The General Assembly discussed the question of creating nuclear-weapon-free zones in areas adjoining the Indian Ocean in 1974 and 1975. Resolutions to that effect were passed concerning Africa, the Middle East or

West Asia and South Asia. An attempt was made to link the creation of nuclear-weapon-free zones in the area with question like removing the foreign presence, creation of a Peace Zone and the denuclearization in the Indian Ocean. In this connection, the Sri Lanka delegate, while speaking before the First Committee of the General Assembly on 11 November 1974, said that not all the nuclear threshold countries in the Indian Ocean region seemed ready or willing to accede to the non-proliferation treaty, and that if a new nuclear-weapon power were to emerge in the Indian Ocean region, the denuclearization and also the demilitarization of the area would be seriously jeopardized.[13]

It would be a wrong tactic on the part of the Indian Ocean states to link the question of the removal of the foreign presence in the Indian Ocean to the question of creation of nuclear-weapon-free zones in the area. India is supposed to be a nuclear threshold country and it has already exploded a nuclear device. But India has not produced a bomb and it does not wish to be a nuclear-weapon power. Secondly, while India has openly declared its intention not to produce nuclear-weapons and has voted for a Peace Zone in the Indian Ocean, those nuclear-weapon-powers which operate in the Indian Ocean have neither accepted the General Assembly resolutions nor have paid any heed to the requests of the Ad Hoc Committee to discuss the question of foreign presence in the area.

The other suggestion to combat the foreign presence in the Indian Ocean area is to neutralize a given region. The ASEAN is deeply involved in it. The idea was projected by the Malaysian Prime Minister, Tun Abdul Razak, during the Southeast Asian Ministerial Conference for the Economic Development of Southeast Asia, which was held at Kuala Lumpur in May 1971. He said that the countries of Southeast Asia would give notice to the Great Powers of their intention to chart their own futures, and determine their own destinies, that they would have no part in the world power game, and that they would not be used, willingly or unwillingly, as pawns. He asked China, the U.S.A. and the U.S.S.R. to jointly guarantee the neutrality of the region. The plan was supported by the Foreign Ministers of the non-aligned nations in their meeting in New York in September.[14] The ASEAN declaration of 27 November 1971 also said that its members were determined to make the necessary efforts to secure the recognition of, and respect for, Southeast Asia as a Zone of Peace, free from any force or manner of interference from outside powers.[15] The ASEAN also agreed in its meeting at Banguio in June 1973 to formulate procedure for the neutralization of Southeast Asia, and in particular, conditions under which China, Japan, the U.S.A. and the U.S.S.R. were to be asked to respect the proposed neutral zone.

The question of the neutralization of a given area in times of peace poses several problems. In times of war, the question of neutrality is governed by well-established rules of international law. A state can declare its neutrality and hope that it would be respected by the belligerent states. But neutrality, in the context of the Cold War or a no-war situation, is a political question and not subject to any well-defined principles of international law or even international relations. In the absence of regional solidarity, the neutralization of Southeast Asia would depend merely upon the goodwill of the foreign powers. If the question were to be settled between the two Super Powers only, there still would have been some chance of reaching an understanding between them on that question. But in a region where all the great powers as well as Japan and Australia are deeply involved such a chance in infinitesimal. Even if some arrangement is agreed upon, the question still remains as to who would guarantee it. Such a guarantee cannot come from outside, not even from the United Nations. Only the local powers, by achieving regional cooperation, can hope to restrain the foreign powers in the region. Hence, it is much more profitable, in the long run, to work for a regional cooperation rather than seek neutrality under dubious guarantees of foreign powers.

The third suggestion regarding limiting foreign presence in the Indian Ocean is to negotiate for a balanced Super Power presence in the area. The idea is finding support in the U.S.A. and Australia. Some littoral states like Sri Lanka are also indirectly supporting it. Amerasinghe, while speaking before an informal meeting of the U.N. Ad Hoc Committee on the Indian Ocean on 16 April 1973, said that even under any agreement for nuclear disengagement in the Indian Ocean, the powers may not renounce the right of transit of any type of warship including submarines, and they would probably wish to maintain enemy submarine surveillance and detection devices to ensure compliance with any agreement on disengagement in the area. He said that the littoral states should consider how their rights could be exercised in a manner consistent with the objective of establishing a Peace Zone in the Indian Ocean.[16]

The littoral states have understood and, to some extent, have taken advantage of the inner contradictions in the communist world, but they look at the West as a monolithic bloc. If the inner contradictions among the Western countries are utilized by the littoral states, it would not be difficult to elicit the support of at least some of them. This division in the West was revealed very sharply in the case of the Arab-Israeli dispute and also in their response in the challenges posed by the Arab oil embargo and the increase in the oil price. The oil weapon that has been so successfully used in the case of the Arab-Israeli conflict can also be used to create a Peace Zone in the Indian Ocean. The oil producing countries in the Gulf can play a major role in this respect. They are already working towards creating a regional understanding to eliminate the foreign presence from the Gulf. They must actively pursue their policy, even beyond the Gulf, and use their political and economic pressure to create a Peace Zone in the Indian Ocean. Because of the oil weapon, they have the power to win over France and Great Britain to their side. They are no longer powers that cannot be managed by the littoral states. If isolated from the U.S.A. they can be useful to the emerging countries in the area in their attempt to break away from the bipolarity created by the Super Powers. Their cooperation would also be useful to these developing countries in their effort to reach the take-off stage in the economic field.

All these options are conditional upon one major fact; the evolution of the concept of an Indian Ocean Community. Almost all the littoral and hinterland states agree upon the need for evolving such a community.. Efforts are being made in Southeast Asia and the Gulf to give shape to it on a regional level. It can start with economic cooperation and finally lead to politico-military understanding. If the littoral states take positive steps towards the evolution of an Indian Ocean Community, they would not only pave the way for the creation of a Peace Zone in the Indian Ocean, but would also lay the foundation of mutual cooperation and economic prosperity in this vital and sensitive area.

Indian Ocean Peace

The Indian Ocean has become a dangerous flashpoint of international tension. In addition to Diego Garcia, the U.S. is pressing for springboards on the territories of Sri Lanka, Pakistan and other countries of the region. It is now nurturing plans to deploy first-strike Pershing-2 missiles in the region. People are particularly alarmed by Washington's plans to use the bases in the Indian Ocean in the 'Star Wars' programme. The specially set-up Central Command (CENTCOM), which is charged with planning and guiding punitive operations of the American military in the Indian Ocean and the Persian Gulf area, is at present drawing up measures to implement the American space militarisation programme in the region.

The unrestrained military expansion of the United States is causing grave alarm not only among the littoral states, but also among most of the U.N. members. In 1971, the international community of nations adopted the Declaration on Turning the Indian Ocean into a Zone of Peace. Its underlying principles are : to eliminate the foreign military bases in the area, to end the arms race, to ban deployment of nuclear weapons, to renounce the threat and use of force against the sovereignty, territorial integrity and independence of the developing countries situated there. But these principles did not suit the ruling quarters in the United States, which, under Reagan's doctrine of new-globalism sought to establish in this vast region their military-political domination.

The Indian Ocean is also strategically important. Sea and air routes run across it linking Europe, East Africa, the Middle East, South and Southeast Asia, the Far East, Australia and Oceania. The Indian Ocean, 'connecting' the Atlantic and Pacific Oceans, is a major hub of sea communications (third place in the world in the volume of sea shipping). The network of waterways is denser here than anywhere else in the world. Air lines stretching over the Indian Ocean have also become significant. Their total length exceeds one million kilometers. Of the world's 240 airports serving inter-continental air routes, about a third are in the Indian Ocean countries.

As for Russia, it used the Indian Ocean from ancient times. In 1466 the Russian merchant Afanasii Nikitin, after going down the Volga and then across the Caspian, crossed Iran and via the Indian Ocean reached India where he spent almost three years, leaving mankind his diary 'A Journey Beyond Three Seas'. Having come across the diary in the middle of the 19th century, the great Russian historian N.M. Karamzin wrote: "Up until now geographers have not known that the credit of one of the most ancient record of European travels to Indian belongs to Russia.....While Vasco da Gama only thought of finding a possible route from Africa to Hindustan, our man from Tyer (Afanasii Nikitin was born there; the city is now Kalinin) was already travelling on the Malabar Coast....." Nikitin's mission was commercial and peaceful. In short, Russians sailed in the Indian Ocean even before the discovery of America. Such are historical facts.

The determination of the new national states to play an ever more active role in world politics and to withstand imperialism's designs together gave rise to one of the biggest positive movements in contemporary history — the movement of non-alignment, now incorporating over 100 countries with a total population of 1.5 billion. It was the Indian Ocean countries that were in the majority among the founders of this movement. Having 'grown literally from the depths of the Indian Ocean', the Non-aligned Movement possesses a great peace potential. In the Political Declaration adopted by the 7th Conference of Heads of State and Government of Non-Aligned Nations in New Delhi in 1983 it was noted that "ever since the Lusaka Summit Confernece first called upon all States to consider and respect the Indian Ocean as a Zone of Peace, non-aligned States have consistently extended their unanimous support to the Declaration of the Indian Ocean as a Zone of Peace.....The non-aligned countries are determined to work for the success of the Conference of the Indian Ocean". They urged the United Nations' Ad Hoc Committee to complete its preparations for the Conference strictly in accordance with its mandate.

The leaders of non-aligned countries, gathered in New Delhi, expressed their "full support" for Mauritian sovereignty over the Chagos archipelago, including Diego Garcia which was detached from the territory of Mauritius by the former colonial power in 1965 in contravention of United Nations General

Assembly Resolutions 1514 (XV) and 2055 (XX). The establishment and strengthening of the military base of Diego Garcia had endangered the sovereignty, territorial integrity and peaceful development of Mauritius and other States. They called for the early return of Diego Garcia to Mauritius.

The Conference of Heads of States and Government of non-aligned nations in Harare was a major opportunity for the Non-Aligned Movement to raise its voice in the struggle for peaceful waters of the Indian Ocean.

Characteristically, it was in the Indian Ocean that the United States and other Western countries faced a resolute attempt by newly-free states to end the existing system of imperialist exploitation based on uncontrolled domination on the part of Western monopolies. In the beginning of the seventies, oil-rich Indian Ocean states united into an Organisation of Petroleum Exporting Countries (OPEC). Having nationalised oil, they turned from being an object of the oil policy of imperialism into a force actively resisting it.

And yet, even at the end of the eighties the situation in the Indian Ocean was not yet relatively tense. The military presence of non-coastal states was comparatively limited. It then seemed that the process of detente could be extended to this area as well. In this context the Soviet Union started negotiations with the U.S.A. on limiting and subsequently reducing the military activity here.

Four rounds of talks took place from June 1977 to February 1978. The talks proceeded encouragingly. The sides agreed to approach the question of reducing military activity in the Indian Ocean on a step-by-step basis; first not to increase their military presence, and then go over to its curtailments. They agreed on some points of a future cut and, what was more, reached an understanding that new military bases would not be created in the area and that the U.S. base at Diego Garcia and in Berbera (Somalia) would be dismantled. But in February 1979, the U.S. unilaterally broke off the talks and, in spite of the repeated proposals of the Soviet Union, never came back to the negotiating table again. By then the U.S.A. had already completed a plan for its strategic uses of the Indian Ocean, allocating for these purposes 30 billion dollars for 1981-85. The talks on reducing military activity in the Indian Ocean proved to be an obstacle since Washington had been thinking and planning its increase.

The Indian Ocean as a Zone of Peace would certainly enchance security throughout Asia. The Policy Report by the C.P.S.U. Central committee to the 57th C.P.S.U. Congress mentioned, among the necessary and useful steps taken the previous year, the Soviet-Indian summit in Moscow. Its participants stressed the importance the two countries attach to converting the Indian Ocean into a Zone of Peace. The joint Soviet-Indian statement said : "The Soviet Union and India express concern over the further complication of the situation in the Indian Ocean and call for closing all foreign military bases in the region and not allowing the establishment of new bases. They are also against any attempts to increase the foreign military presence in the Indian Ocean. The Sides stand for early implementation of the U.N. General Assembly to immediately call a conference on the Indian Ocean into a Zone of Peace and support the decision by the U.N. Declaration on turning the Indian Ocean into a Zone of Peace and support the decision by the U.N. General Assembly to immediately call a conference on the Indian Ocean for the purpose. The Soviet Union decisively backs the striving of India and other non-aligned countries to reach this objective."[17]

Along with the idea of a Peace Zone for the Indian Ocean, a whole number of constructive initiatives on other aspects of Asian security have been advanced in recent years. In 1981 the Soviet Union proposed discussing confidence-building measures for the Far East, similar to those which are being implemented in Europe on the basis of the 1975 Helsinki agreements. The Mongolian People's Republic suggested concluding a convention on mutual non-aggression and non-use of force by countries in Asia and the Pacific. The states of Indochina are steadily working to make South-East Asia a zone of peace, stability and co-operation. A better situation in the Far East would be promoted by implementing the proposals of the Democratic People's Republic of Korea to withdraw American troops from South Korea and to reunite the country on the basis of peaceful and democratic principles without outside interference.

The US Policy Postures

The United States of America has been pursuing a policy of extending her influence over South Asian region since the inception of this region's freedom from colonial rule. It has been repeatedly asserted by some that South Asia occupies a low priority area in the US scheme of things. These assertions, however, do not conform to the real state of affairs and actual policy being practised by the USA in this region. Having taken over the mantle of protecting the interests in the erstwhile colonies of British and French colonial empires, the USA came in a big way in South and South East Asian region to fill in the so-called vacuum that had supposedly been created owing to the withdrawal of these two countries. This vacuum theory was sought to be justified in the name of 'containing communism', and a series of military pacts came into existence around South and South East Asian regions and West Asia. Some countries of the regions fell a prey to the temptation of protection and security that these pacts ostensibly offered, and joined them. In fact, these pacts sponsored by the USA were manifestations of last-ditch attempts to stem the tide of national liberation. These pacts provided protection, not so much against external aggression, but in maintaining pliable, status-quoist and oppressive regimes in those countries which joined them.

Taking advantage of the continuing conflict between the Soviet Union and China, the US devised the strategy of building a new balance of power against the forces of anti-imperialism and the Soviet Union, leaving South East Asia for the Chinese to take care, and herself concentrating on South Asian, South West and West Asian regions. Speaking particularly of the South Asian scenario, one finds Pakistan, having acted as a conduit between China and the USA, becoming the kingpin in the whole strategy. Hence attempts are afoot from both the US and Chinese sides to strengthen this country militarily in order to make it more subservient to their dictates. The South West Asian situation has,therefore, deliberately been built up to justify large-scale military aid to Pakistan.

In this strategy, the main stumbling block is India, which has consistently rebuffed the Western overtures to fall in line with their policies. Hence the attempts at vitiating the socio-economic and political climate in the country have been intensified to create conditions of destabilization. The aim is to have a pliable and weak political leadership at the helm of affairs and to create conditions of chaos and anarchy. The success of this strategy depends, therefore, on the success of their destabilization attempts. Pakistan plays a crucial role in this game, as has been clearly revealed in the White Paper on the Punjab situation, and in the statements of Mrs. Indira Gandhi and Rajiv Gandhi.

The USA had almost succeeded in her destabilization strategy in 1977 when weak political leaders and military rulers came to power in major South Asian countries like Bangladesh, Pakistan and Sri Lanka. While India's political will reasserted itself by 1980, in Bangladesh and Sri Lanka, governments with definite tilt towards the USA, have continued to remain in power. In the South Asian scenario, these two countries, besides Pakistan, have been playing the US game by projecting what many scholars call the 'small nation psychology'. A kind of 'fear complex' is deliberately being created through different media by accusing India of adopting 'big brotherly' attitude towards her small neighbours on the one hand, and impressing upon the 'small neighbours' the imperative of being on guard against the 'domineering designs' of the 'big neighbour'. The unmistakable call to these small neighbours is to fall in line with the imperialist strategy of destabilizing the big political entity called India, and to come under their umbrella to 'protect their political freedom and territorial integrity' from India's 'aggressive policies'.

The Soviet Policy Postures

As has been stated, the Soviet Union's policy has been motivated by her support to the cause of national independence in erstwhile colonies and to strengthen the forces of anti-imperialism. Since the countries engaged in the tasks of socio-economic emancipation have generally been anti-imperialist, there has emerged a solid basis of friendship and cooperation between the newly independent nations and the Soviet Union. Being fully aware of the growing detente between the United States and China, the Soviet effort is to prevent the expansion of the US influence in developing countries of the world. The task has become all the more important in view of growing Sino-US collusion.

The Soviet support to India's efforts at her own stability and for world peace is part and parcel of her global policy of supporting national liberation movements. The South Asian scenario, however, is not conducive to stability because military and autocratic regimes are at the helm of affairs in some of the South Asian countries. Such regimes constitute a factor of instability in the region which further accentuates the possibilities of imperialist interference.

The Soviet Union is opposed to the US military aid to Pakistan because this only helps to strengthen the military adventure of that country. The regime in Bangladesh too does not enjoy Soviet support. In view of the persistent rumour about the possibility of granting military base at Chittagong to the United States, the Soviet-Bangladesh relations have further been strained. Both Pakistan and Bangladesh have been contributing their bit to the process of destabilization in India and this has not been looked with favour in Moscow. Sri Lanka's internal problems and failure of the Jayawardene government to resolve the ethnic issue made this country extremely vulnerable to imperialist machinations. Her increasing anti-Indian stand and hostility towards the Soviet Union have put her in the category of Pakistan and Bangladesh. In such a situation, the Soviet Union would not like to leave the region absolutely open for the imperialist powers. Hence her policy is to strengthen India as a factor of stability in South Asia and to try to convince India's neighbours that they should work for reforming their own political and socio-economic structures by making them truly democratic and participatory in nature.

In sum, it may be pointed out that the presence of Super Powers in the Indian Ocean is a fact which should be reckoned with. While responding to this fact, it is necessary not to equate the two Super Powers, as their motives in the area are totally different from each other. We must recognise that this rivalry is an extension of the conflict between the forces of imperialism and anti-imperialism. Instead of responding collectively to a serious situation, they are working at cross purposes, thus further accentuating the disease for the cure of which they profess to be seriously concerned. In this context to talk in terms of cooperation among the littoral countries seems to be unrealistic. Cooperation emanates from identity of views and similarities in perceptions. This crucial factor is nowhere to be seen in South Asia.

Prospects in the Indian Ocean

Despite divergent interests and contradictory alignments, the Indian Ocean states have supported all moves proposing the Indian Ocean as a Zone of Peace (IOZP). The Zone of Peace proposal has largely been motivated by a common fear that strategic competition between the Super Powers in the area would affect regional autonomy, independence and co-operation. It is generally believed that the full-time presence of external powers in the Indian Ocean region has contributed to littoral fears that the interventionist capabilities of the Super Powers might encourage military solutions to the local conflict.[18]

Local apprehensions about the naval arms race and the extension of extra-regional rivalry in the Indian Ocean were expressed as early as 1964, at the second conference of non-aligned countries in Cairo. The Conference condemned all attempts by the Super Powers to seek domination in Africa and Asia, and recommended the establishment of denuclearised zones covering the world's oceans.[19] In the late 1950s and early 1960s, a variety of nuclear-free zone proposals had already been put forward at international fora for Latin America, Central Europe, Africa and the Southern Hemisphere. The most relevant of these earlier suggestions to the current IOZP movement was a proposal from Sri Lanka in 1964 for a nuclear free zone in the Indian Ocean. In the same year the Soviet Union proposed the creation of nuclear-free zones in the Indian Ocean and the Mediterranean.[20]

The pursuit of non-aligned policies by a large number of littoral states, and more importantly, the prospects of detente between the Super Powers, encouraged the proponents of the Peace Zone. It was during the Lusaka Conference of the non-aligned nations in 1970 that the IOZP concept was finally developed and articulated. The final communique of the Conference adopted a declaration designating the Indian Ocean as a

Zone of Peace free of nuclear weapons and Great Power rivalries.

All the major maritime powers agreed to the IOZP proposal in principle, but opposed efforts by the littoral states to exclude warships from the adjacent areas. They argued that the establishment of special legal regimes would constitute an unacceptable departure from the long-standing rules of inter-national law concerning the freedom of navigation in the high seas.[21] The Super Powers also rejected and continue to reject co-operation with the U.N. measures to implement the Peace Zone resolutions. A variety of factors explain the resistance of the Super Powers to the IOZP proposals. In part, it represents the traditional opposition of maritime powers to any restriction on the use of the seas. Having the capacity to project sea power in the region, the Soviet Union and the United States are unwilling to forego the diplomatic and political advantages of their naval presence, which they have been strengthening by deploying more ships and acquiring an extensive network of port facilities in the region.

The Indian Ocean has emerged as an important area of naval deployments for the Super Powers, albeit for different reasons. The principal American concern in the area has been access to the Persian Gulf oil, whereas the Soviet Union has centred her focus on expanding political and security influence, primarily among the neutral and anti-west states. Both the Soviet and American policy-makers have argued that Peace Zone proposals would deny them a legitimate right to deploy forces on behalf of their interests. Despite acceptance of the developing nations' claims at the Law of the Sea Conference for a 12-mile territorial limit and a 200-mile exclusive zone, the Super Powers have refused to countenance claims by the Indian Ocean states to regulate the 'innocent passage' of warships in these areas. Contrary to the existing legal position of the movement of military shipping, the African and Asian states do not subscribe to 'any definition of the freedom of the seas as implying the right to create conditions of anarchy, to roam at free will threatening all and sundry'.[22]

The Super Powers complained that their naval activities in the Indian Ocean were singled out for undue criticism. The

Americans expressed annoyance at the one-sided comments of the littoral states specifically directed against them. The U.S. has argued that her naval presence has been castigated more often than that of the Soviets.[23] The Soviet Union, on the other hand, complained that the non-aligned states unwarrantedly equated their naval activity with that of the United States, claiming that the Soviet presence has been beneficial to the progressive political forces in the region. As a political strategy, the Soviet Union insisted on the dismantling of 'foreign bases' and 'imperial presence' in the Indian Ocean rather than placing prohibitions on the deployment of 'foreign naval forces'.[24] In this effort the Soviets succeeded, through their supporters at the Non-Aligned Conference in Colombo in August 1976, in including the elimination of 'existing foreign bases' in the peace zone resolution.[25] Obviously, it was aimed at the American supply base at Diego Garcia. The declaration of the last Non-aligned Summit Conference held in Delhi in 1983 was balanced in calling for 'reduction and eventual elimination' of the Super Powers' military presence in the Indian Ocean.[26]

The Ad Hoc Committee on the Indian Ocean which was established in 1972 also submitted a report on the implementation of the IOZP declaration.[27] The Committee report suggested, among other provisions, that it be transformed into a negotiating forum to facilitate consultations with the Super Powers on all issues relating to the demilitarisation of the Indian Ocean. In addition, it also recommended a conference of the littoral and hinterland states of the Indian Ocean as an essential step towards the relaxation of tension and furthering the cause of the peace-zone declaration.[28] The proposed international conference on the Indian Ocean designed to criticise the naval build-ups of the external powers evoked little enthusiasm from the United States and the Soviet Union.

The Indian Ocean states have regularly discussed the naval escalation of the Super Powers and its security impact on the region, including the Zone of Peace issue. Since 1972, the IOZP proposal has been kept alive in the Ad Hoc Committee of the Indian Ocean. The Committee's membership has steadily swelled to 47, including littoral states, permanent members of the Security Council, with China, Greece and Japan and some others also joining as major maritime users of the ocean. The Committee holds a series of meetings each year and prepares its resolution on the IOZP, so ritually passed by the U.N. General Assembly.

The Ad Hoc Committee on the Indian Ocean met several times in February 1981 to consider ways of implementing the IOZP declaration and to discuss the question of convening a conference on the Indian Ocean scheduled for that year in Colombo, as stipulated by the December 1979 resolution. During the 1980-81 Ad Hoc Committee sessions. Since then, the Western countries have expressed the view that there are several matters of substance relating to the implementation of the Indian Ocean Peace Zone declaration, including a deterioration of the international situation in the region brought about, in particular, by the presence of Soviet forces in Afghanistan.

In the wake of regional tensions, and the subsequent naval build-up by the Super Powers, Soviet President Brezhnev proposed a 'Doctrine of Peace and Security' for the Perisan Gulf during his December 1980 visit to India. The proposed five-point doctrine called for an agreement not to set up foreign military bases in the Persian Gulf area and on adjacent islands; not to deploy nuclear or any other weapons of mass destruction there; not to use force against the countries of the Persian Gulf area; not to interfere in their internal affairs; and to respect the status of non-alignment of the Gulf states. Brezhnev's peace doctrine was not received as a credible gesture in the face of the Soviet occupation of Afghanistan. More than a peace doctrine, it was seen as a diplomatic offensive against the U.S. naval presence in the area.

The regional powers lack consensus on the issue of demilitarisation of the Indian Ocean. Failure to convene a much delayed conference for the consideration of IOZP proposal due to the deadlock in the Ad Hoc Committee of the Indian Ocean, clearly explains limitations of the regional powers. For all practical purposes, diplomatic pressures and initiatives at international forums such as the U.N. and the Non-aligned Movement (NAM) have failed to influence the Indian Ocean policies of the Super Powers. The regional states have wide differences of opinion on security issues, including the presence of the Super Powers' forces in one or another form. The political use of maritime power by the Super Powers to achieve national objectives is another reason for the lack of any progress in demilitarisation or arms reduction proposals in the Indian Ocean region.

The Super Powers perceive their economic and strategic interests in the Indian Ocean to be so vital that it seems unrealistic to expect them to agree to total demilitarisation. Nor is there any substance in the argument that once the Super Power relinquish their facilities and withdraw their navies, the Indian Ocean region would instantly become a zone of peace. The regional power politics, rivalries and militarisation of littoral states is, of course, as menacing to peace as coveting influence and protecting interests through power projection capabilities by the external powers. The geopolitics of the Indian Ocean has increasingly grown more complex both by power ambitions of regional states and significant additions to the U.S. and Soviet naval capabilities in recent years.

REFERENCES

1. J.C. Caldwell in A. Kerr (ed.), *The Indian Ocean Region: Resources and Development,* 1981, p. 17.
2. *Economic and Political Weekly,* (Bombay), 11.4.1981, p. 640.
3. James Schlesinger, "Third World Conflict and International Security in the 1980's", *Survival,* Nov. - Dec., 1980, pp. 274-81; and R.W. Tucker, "The Purposes of American Power", in *Foreign Affairs*, Winter, 1980, pp. 241-74.
4. John Erickson, *Afghanistan : The Soviet Invasion and its Consequences for the British Policy,* London, 1980, p. 253.
5. Dieter Braun, *op. cit.* at n. 12, p. 67.
6. Report of U.S. Senate Committee, *op. cit.,* at n. 6.
7. *New York Times,* 12 January 1968.
8. V. Matveyer, "Stuffed Vacuum", *Izvestia* (MOSCOW), 28 May, 1971.
9. Two of his books deserve special mention; *The Influence of Sea Power Upon History 1660-1783,* Boston, 1890; and *Naval Stratgy,* Boston, 1911. Other writers have further elaborated the theme and written on the topic. Some of these works are H.W. Richmont,

Sea Power in the Modern World, London, 1934; and S.W. Roskill, *The Strategy of Sea Power, Its Development and Application*, Ontario, 1962.

10. A/C. 1/PV 1836, 25 November, 1971, p. 30.
11. A/AC. 159/L. 3 included in A/9021 (XXVIII), p. 25.
12. *The Hindu* and *The Hindustan Times,* 5 March, 1974.
13. A/C. 1/PV, 2015, 11 November, 1974, p. 12.
14. A/C. 1/PV. 1836, 25 November, 1971, p. 30.
15. A/C. 1/PV. 1840, 30 November, 1971, p. 30.
16. U.N. Ad Hoc Committee Report 1973 A/9029, p. 26.
17. Yevgeni Rumyantsev, *Indian Ocean and Asian Security,* New Delhi, Allied, 1986, pp. 45-53.
18. V.R. Krishna Iyer, 'Indian Ocean and Jurisprudence of Peace', *Mainstream Weekly* (Annual 1982).
19. Conference of Heads of States and Governments of Non-aligned Countries, Cairo, October 5-10, 1964 (Cairo : A Ministry of National Guidance Publications, 1964), pp. 350-2.
20. UNGA Official Records, 19th Session, Annexes, no. 9, Document A/5827, Letter dated 7 December, 1964, from the Minister for Foreign Affairs of the Union of Soviet Socialist Republics to the President of the General Assembly.
21. U.S. Congress, Diego Garcia, 1975 : Debate Over the Base and The Island's Former Inhabitants, p. 4.
22. UNGA, 26th Session, First Committee Debate, 1 December 1971. A/CI/pv 1842, p. 4. The statement by Amer Singhe, the Sri Lankan representative.
23. U.S. Congress, Senate Committee on Armed Forces. Disapprove Construction Projects on the Island of Diego Garcia, 1975, p. 62.
24. Kin Beazley, 'The Indian Ocean : A Triumph of Interest over Ideal', *Dissent,* 35, 36 (Autumn/Winter 1977), p. 32.
25. *Review of International Affairs,* 5 September, 1976, p. 28.
26. For the text of the Summit declaration, see *Asian Recorder,* 16-22 April, 1983, pp. 17128-31.
27. U.N. Ad Hoc Committee on the Indian Ocean, Official Records, 29th Session, supplement no. 29 A/9629.
28. UNGA, Resolution 3259 (XXIX).

CHAPTER VII

Epilogue

Socialism stands dismantled today in the USSR and Eastern Europe. The response and perception of the Third World countries to these dramatic events was generally similar. The USSR was considered an ally. With the disintegration of the USSR, bipolarism international politics seems to have come to an end. As a result, the US has got an opportunity to extend its hegemony and to convert the world into a unipolar entity.

The US, by partially applying Special 301 to India and pressurising her to toe the Dunkel Draft, expects her to accept the conditions laid down by IMF and World Bank for loans. A similar attempt was made when action was taken against Russia for agreeing to transfer cryogenic rocket technology to India on the pretext of maintaining balance of power in the Indian ocean region. The sanction, in the form of a two-year ban on American trade and technology transfers with and to the ISRO and Glavkosmos, is a punitive action against India and Russia for 'violating' the guidelines of the Missile Technology Control Regime. In the US world-view, it should be the only Super Power and in its scheme of things the system of checks and balances does not find a place. Countries which have not signed the Nuclear Non-proliferation Treaty are being pressurised to fall in line. With the threat of confrontation with the Soviet Union receding, Centcom's strategy now seems to be the protection of West Asian Oil and to maintain military balance to prevent countries like India from emerging stronger. India has been trying to get some kind of guarantee from both the nuclear and non-nuclear countries before signing the NPT. It was made ample clear as early as 4 December, 1964 by the then Prime Minister, Lal Bahadur Shastri during his visit to

London. When he demanded such guarantees of security. This was reiterated by M.C. Chagla on 12 April, 1967 when he declared that India wanted "a joint guarantee from both the US and the Soviet Union against the nuclear attack". The Resolution 255 of the Security Council passed on June 19th, 1968 included, inter alia, Security assurances to only those countries which signed the NPT which made India wary of signing it.

It has been rightly observed that the US won a low cost and low casuality victory in the Gulf War while the USSR was collapsing and the Communist regimes in East Europe were disintegrating. As a result, the US became the only Super Power in the world with a one-dimensional view of the international situation. A draft document prepared by Paul D. Wolfowidz, the Pentagon's Under Secretary for Policy, in February 1992, invited global attention. The documents stressed the need for creating a world dominated solely by the US and asking for a "base force" sanction for 1.6 million army in five years' time at a cost of $1.2 trillion. The deployment of the US army for the prevention of proliferation of nuclear weapons was also envisaged. The document mentions India as a possible hegemonistic power in South Asia. In fact, the old idea of the US playing the role of the 'global policeman' was revived. V.P. Dutt in his article "Whither Indo-US Ties" rightly points out that "in restructuring Indo-US relations, New Delhi must keep in view this duality of the American reality and neither underestimate the US needs and pressures nor to be continually over-awed by them... New Delhi must also fully appreciate the duality of its own situation. Temporarily India is in a messy economic situation and must bend skillfuly in order to rise again... India has many sources of strength and need not confuse accommodation with capitulation".

In a debate on "Indian Foriegn Policy in the Changing World" held on April 27th, 1992 at New Delhi, S. Viswam, an eminent journalist, expressed the view that the world was always a multi-polar one. It was the crumbling of an important pole which was the cause of concern. M.K. Rasgotra, former Secretary in the Ministry of External Affairs, was of the view that it would not help to ignore Russia whatever be the polarity today because it continued to be a major military power.

In a debate of India's Foreign Policy in the Lok Sabha on 20th April, 1992, members made a strong plea for review India's Foreign Policy in view of the changing international scenario. It was emphasised that even in the changed world situation the basic concept of non-alignment was still relevant and India should continue to strengthen NAM and SAARC. Concern was expressed about the fall out of developments in Afghanistan. Jaswant Singh, M.P., while commenting on the establishment of diplomatic relations with Israel, talked of the double standard of the US in matter of Pak-inspired terrorism and nuclear weapons programme. He wanted the government to draw the attention of the US about these 'irritants' in our relations. The proposed joint naval exercise with the US was considered as an about-turn in the country's foreign policy and several members felt that it would expose India's sensitive areas and information to the US.

The Tirupati Resolution of the Congress on International Affairs, in May, 1992, reaffirms "independence of judgement" and "autonomy of decision making in external relations" as the basic principles of India's Foreign Policy. There are clear indication of shifting of emphasis from West and South Asia to other Asian countries like Japan and China. It is felt that the revival of India's ties with South-East Asian countries will help in strengthening the Indian Ocean Security and will be economically beneficial to both the sides.

The US also needs new allies for safeguarding her interests in the Asian-Pacific region with her growing economic, political and security stakes. India's position in the Indian Ocean region is unrivalled because of her geostrategic importance. Prime Minister Narasimha Rao has rightly pointed out, "We must sustain our self-confidence. We must realise that India is not just another state but a state that constitutes a civilisation centre... secure in its inner strength. It is that inner source of strength and grandeur that we must be able to touch in the struggles that we continue to face".

If reports from Washington are to be believed, the Pentagon has already revised its "defence planning guidance" for 1994-99 which is less aggressive and omits the reference to India's hegemonic aspirations in South Asia. Instead, Defence

Secretary Richard Cheney referred to collective military action and preservation and expansion of the system of alliances as a key feature of the US strategy.

Indo-US relations have entered a crucial phase of negotiations. Since India is out of the Soviet orbit, the US is taking a fresh look at India. The possibilities are immense. India can be crucial and strategic partner in the Indian Ocean and a potential market for investments besides being a counterveiling force to China. This is evident in the stance taken by the US on Kashmir, almost totally supporting India in her longstanding dispute with Pakistan. The Kickleighter proposals of April, 1991 advocated "expanded strategic co-operation" between the India and the US armed forces. The thawing of Indo-US relations is also evident from the joint naval exercise in the Indian Ocean that took place in May, 1992. Four Warships—two destroyers and two frigates — carried out joint manoeuverses over a two-day period in the Indian Ocean. When former Warsaw Pact countries like Romania can exercise with the US navy, and India can do it with the British or the French navies, it is illogical not to do the same with the US which is one of the most professional navies in the world. The exercise was meant to test each other's reaction time and response. Since the US has realised the importance of the shipping lanes which pass through the Indian Ocean, the role of India assumes critical importance. The US has also realised that India could act as a buffer in the event of a possible conflict with China or in West Asia. Some defence analysts even visualise the possibility of the US aid for the building of Karwar Naval Base which is a window to the Indian Ocean. With economic liberalization India is already on the road to improve its ties with the West.

As far as China is concerned, it can no longer play the US against the USSR or viceversa. It wants to resist the pressures of the US in such areas has missile technology control and trade. It is therefore, keen to improve relations with India, to mend fences with Vietnam and improve economic relations with Japan and other Third World countries. President Venkataraman's visit to China in May, 1992 was described by President Yang Shangkun as "laying the foundation for long-term cooperation between the two countries on a stronger and more durable basis".

With the end of the cold war it is being asked whether NAM is still relevant. It is suggested that since the main problems being faced by the developing countries are economic, NAM should merge with G-77. While the new international scenario demands a change in priorities and emphasis, the continuity of NAM is desirable because many issues faced by the Third World countries are still unresolved. Romesh Bhandari, former Secretary, External Affairs, in his article "The Relevance of NAM" points out that "collective political pressure will need to be exerted in international" force on the clear linkage between disarmament, development and international stability. This NAM alone can do.

The tenth Non-Aligned Summit opened in Jakarata on 1 September, 1992 with a forceful plea by President Shuarto of Indonesia for rejection of loans having strings attached to them and for evolving consensus on the strategy for the economic growth of the developing countries. He also called for creating a support mechanism to implement the agreements reached on South-South co-operation.

He also talked about the current international political situation. "So long as world peace is endangered, the freedom of nations diminished, the fundamental aspirations of the people reduced, and economic injustices continue, so long shall the NAM have to be in the forefront of struggle to oppose them. We must also ensure that the new world order to which the leaders of the industrialised countries often refer, does not turn out to be but a new version of the same old patterns of domination of the strong over the weak and the rich over the poor."

The U.N. Secretary-General, Boutros Ghali underlined the parallelism that existed between the objectives of NAM and the U.N. These are : non-alignment in East-West confrontation, alignment with respect to anti-colonial struggles, non-participation in multilateral military alliances, non-participation in any bilateral alliance with a Super Power and refusal to accommodate the military base of a Super Power.

In a hard-hitting speech on the second day of the Tenth Non-aligned Summit Prime Minister P.V.Narasimha Rao said the over-growing list of items subjected to so-called dual-use restrictions effectively threatened to deprive the developing countries of the fruits of technological progress in many key areas.

Stressing the paramount importance of South-South cooperation, the Prime Minister said developing countries must themselves learn to recognise their own capacities and the south must respect the south as a first step towards cooperation among them.

He said the G-15 was born out of the compelling need for self-reliance to enable the non-aligned countries to harness the immense resources of talent and skill inherent in their people and it had now established itself as a core around which the NAM could promote South-South cooperation.

Speaking about the ecological balance that was closely linked to increase of resources, Mr.Rao called upon the NAM to establish a mechanism to make concrete recommendations for establishing a planet protection fund proposed by Rajiv Gandhi at the 1989 Belgrade NAM summit. Speaking about the democratisation of the international order, he stressed the need for a non-confrontationalist, yet decisive North-South dialogue.

He said that the approaches of the North and the South to economic problems were bound to be different and only a dialogue could bring home the fact of interdependence and the indispensability of viable solutions. Expressing concern at the decline of multilateralism, he called for reactivating consultative mechanisms at all multilateral fora to halt the "slide into a world of persistent monologue."

A draft declaration to the Tenth NAM Summit calls upon all member-States to refrain from organising, instigating, assisting or participating in terrorist act in or against other countries.

The draft, circulated by host Indonesia, deems it important to distinguish between State-sponsored terrorism that poses a threat to international peace and "desperate acts committed by individual due to the denial of freedom, justice and fair-play". On international trade and commodities, the draft declaration identifies free access to the developed countries makrets as an indispensable means of taking full advantage of international trade.

The draft emphasises that the results of the Urugay Round of Multilateral Trade Negotiations (URMTN) should be fully responsive to the special needs of the non-aligned and other developing countries and conducive to the integration of their economies into the mainstream of the world economy.

The draft deals with the role of the NAM in the emerging new international order and says that the changes would not alter or diminish the validity of the basic principles and objectives of the movement.

"Today, the movement remains vindicated as ideological and military blocs have crumbled and an era of cooperation has dawned." it emphasises.

The tenth Non-Aligned Summit, which concluded in Jakarta on 6 September, 1992, gave the call for a new world order based on a collective commitment to peace and assuring a just and equitable social and economic order. The conference also adopted the *'Jakarta Message'* suggesting co-ordination of NAM efforts with Group 77. It noted that the collapse of the bi-polar structure of the world presented unprecedented possibilities, as well challenges, for co-operation among nations. It envisaged a world free from nuclear weapons which alone could ensure human survival. Grave concern was expressed about the tendency of Big Powers to intervene in the internal affairs of other states under the pretext of protecting human rights or preventing conflict and called for full respect for the sovereignty of nations. The Jakarta Summit proved that while NAM will have to undergo a process of readjustment in a post-Soviet world, it continued to be a movement for independence from colonial masters, steering clear of military alliances. There was consensus among nations for shunning state-sponsored terrorism and for evolving regional mechanisms to resolve bilateral disputes. It was noted that the indebtedness of the developing countries had doubled over a decade from \$ 700 billion in 1981 to \$ 1400 billion in 1992. A call was given for the setting up of a mechanism to help resolve the chronic indebtedness of many developing countries since it stifles their growth. While not deviating from its basis politicial objectives, NAM is sought to be given a specific economic content to sustain and strengthen the movement.

Bangladesh has recently mooted the idea of establishing a SAARC parliament in order to create some kind of a South Asian identity to shape and strengthen the political, economic, cultural and geographical contours of the Association in the minds of the people of the region.

It is hoped that the concerted efforts on the part of the Third World countries would ultimately lead to the evolution of the Indian Ocean Community and the Indian Ocean would truly become a Zone of Peace.

Bibliography

BOOKS

Adie, W.A.C., *Oil, Politics and Seapower : The Indian Ocean Vortex*. New York : Crane, Russak, 1975.

Alford, Jonathan, ed., *Sea Power and Influence : Old Issues and New Challenges*. Montclair, N.J. : Cover and Allanhed, Osmun, 1980.

Amirie, A., ed., *The Persian Gulf and Indian Ocean in International Politics*. Tehran : Institute for International Political and Economic Studies, 1975.

Ballard, G.A., *Rulers of the Indian Ocean*, New York : Houghton Mifflin, 1928.

Barnds, William J., *India, Pakistan, and the Great Powers*. New York : Praeger, for the Council on Foreign Relations, 1974.

Beazley, K.C. and I.Clark, *Politics of Instrusion : The Superpowers and the Indian Ocean*. Sydney : Alternative Publishing Cooperative, 1979.

Bezboruah, Monoranjan, *US Strategy in the Indian Ocean : The International Response*. New York : Praeger, 1977.

Bhagat, G., *Americans in India 1784-1860*. New York : New York University Press, 1970.

Blechman, Barry M., *The Control of Naval Armaments : Prospects and Possibilities*. Studies in Defense Policy. Washington, D.C. : Brookings Institute, 1975.

Booth, Ken, *The Military Instrument in Soviet Foreign Policy 1917-1972*. London : Royal United Services Institute for Defense Studies, 1973.

Bowman, Larry W. and Ian Clark, eds., *The Indian Ocean in Global Politics*. Boulders, Colorado : Westview Press, 1981.

Braun, Dieter, *The Indian Ocean : Region of Conflict or 'Zone of Peace'*. London : C. Hurst & Company, 1983.

Brodie, Bernard, *Strategy and National Interests : Reflections for the Future*. New York : National Strategy Information Center, 1971.

Centori, Louis J. and Steven L. Spiegel, *The International Politics of Regions : A Comparatrive Approach*. Englewood Cliffs, N.J. :Prentice-Hall, 1970.

Carrington, C. E., *The Liquidation of the British Empire*. London : George C. Harrap, 1961.

Centre d'etude du Sud-Est asiatique et de' Extrême Orient, ed. *The Politics of the Great Powers in the Indian Ocean*. Brussels : Free University of Brussels, 1971.

Chapin, William, *The Asian Balance of Power : An American View*. Adelphi Paper no.35. London : Institute for Strategic Studies, April, 1967.

Chestkov, David Gngorevich, *The Soviet Union and Developing Countries : Experience and Prospects of Economic Cooperation*. Moscow : Novosti Press Agency Publication House, 1972.

Choudhury, Golam, W. *Brezhnev's Collective Security Plan for Asia*. North Carolina Central University : Center for Strategic and International Studies, 1976.

———, *India, Pakistan, Bangladesh, and the Major Powers*. New York : Free Press, 1975.

Coffey, Joseph I., *Strategic Power and National Security*. Pittsburgh : University of Pittsburgh Press, 1971.

Cohen, Benjamin J., *The Question of Imperialism : The Political Economy of Dominance and Dependence*. New York : Basic Books, 1973.

Corbett, Julian S., *Some Principles of Maritime Strategy*. New York : Longmans, Green, 1911.

Cottrell, Alvin and Walter F. Hahn, *Indian Ocean Naval Limitations : Regionsl Issues and Global Implications*. New York : National Strategy Information Center, 1976.

Cottrell, Alvin, J. et al., *Sea Power and Strategy in the Indian Ocean*. Beverly Hills : Sage Publications, 1981.

Cottrell, Alvin and R.M. Burreli eds., *The Indian Ocean : Its Political, Economic, and Military Importance.* New York : Praeger, 1972.

Cranwell, John Philips, *The Destiny of Sea Power and its Influence on Land Power and Air Power*, New York : Norton, 1941.

Darby, Phillip, *British Defence Policy East of Suez 1947-1968.* London : Oxford University Press, 1973.

Dil, Shaheen Fatemah., 'Great Power Interaction in Local Crisis : Soviet, American, and Chinese participation in South Asia', Ph.D. Dissertation. Princeton University, 1974.

Donaldson, Robert H., Soviet *Policy toward India: Ideology and Strategy*. Cambridge, Mass. : Harvard University Press, 1974.

Dutt, V.P., *India's Foreign Policy*, Vani Educational Books, New Delhi, 1984

Eldridge, Frank B., *The Background of Eastern Sea Power.* London : Phoenix House, 1948.

Gopal, Madan, *India as a World Power : Aspects of Foreign Policy.* New Delhi : Sansar Publications, 1974.

Gorshkov, S.G., *The Sea Power of the State.* Annapolis, Md. : Naval Institute Press, 1976.

Graham, Gerald S., *Great Britain in the Indian Ocean : A Study of Maritime Enterprise 1810-1850.* Oxford : Oxford University Press, 1967.

———, *The Politics of Naval Supremacy : Studies in British Maritime Ascendancy.* Cambridge : The University Press, 1965.

Gray, Colin S., *The Geopolitics of the Nuclear Era :* Heartland, Rimlands, and the Technological Revolution. New York: Crane, Russak and Co., 1977.

Gupta, Vinod, *Anderson Papers : A Study of Nixon's Blackmail of India.* New Delhi : Indian School Supply Depot, Publication Division, 1972.

Hermann, Clarles F., *New Directions in the Study of Foreign Policy*. Allen and Unwin, Boston, 1987.

Herrick, Carl H., The Indian Ocean : The End of an Era Report no. 3928. 23 March 1970. Air War College, Air University, Alabama : Maxwel Air Force Base, 1970.

Hodson, Henry Vincent, *Twentieth Century Empire*. London : Faber and Faber, 1948.

Hourani, George Fadio, *Arab Seafaring in the Indian Ocean in Ancient and Early Medieval Times*. New York: Octagon Books, 1975.

Hutchinson, Alaister, G.L., The Strategic Significance of the Indian Ocean. Professional Study no. 4619, Air War College, Air University, Alabama : Maxwell Air Force Base, April, 1972.

Indian International Centre, Seminar on Indian Ocean as a Zone of Peace. New Delhi : IIC, 1980.

Jukes, Geoffrey, *The Soviet Union in Asia*. Berkeley : University of California Press, 1973.

Kanet, Roser E. ed., *The Soviet Union and the Developing Nations*. Baltimore : Johns Hopkins University Press, 1974.

Kapur, Ashok, *The Indian Ocean : Regional and International Power Politics*. New York : Praeger, 1982.

Kaul, T.N., *Diplomacy in Peace & War, Recollections and Reflections*. Vikas Publishing House, New Delhi, 1979.

Kaushik, Devendra, *The Indian Ocean : Towards a Peace Zone*. Delhi : Vikas Publications, 1972.

Perspectives on Security in Indian Ocean Region. New Delhi : Allied, 1987.

Khan, Rashid Ahmad, *Scramble for the Indian Ocean*. Lahore: Progressive Publishers, 1973.

Kilmarx, Robert A. ed., *Soviet-United States Naval Balance*. Washington, D.C. : Center for Strategic and International Studies, 1975.

Kincaid, Charles V., *The Energy Crisis and Japan : Future Strategic and Foreign Policy Implications*. Washington, D.C. : National War College, Strategic Research Group, 1975.

Kirkman, William Patrick, *Unscrambling an Empire. A Critique of British Colonial Policy 1956-1966.* London : Chatto & Windus, 1966.

Kumar, Ravinder, *India and the Persian Gulf Region 1858-1907*: A Study in British Imperial Policy. Bombay : Asia Publishing House, 1965.

Kun, Joseph, *Sino-Soviet Competition in Africa : The Crucial Role of Military Assistance.* Munich : Radio Liberty Research, 1976.

Limye, Madhu, *Problems of India's Foreign Policy.* Atma Ram & Sons, Delhi, 1984.

McConnnell, James, ed., *Soviet Naval Diplomacy.* New York : Pergamon, 1979.

McLaurin, Ronald D., *The Soviet Union and the Middle East.* Washington, D.C. : American Institute for Research, Social Environment Research Center, 1974.

Maclean, Donald, *British Foreign Policy since Suez 1956-1968.* London : Hodder and Stoughton, 1970 .

Mahan, A.T., *The Problem of Asia and its Effect Upon International Policies.* Boston : Little Brown, 1900.

— — —, *The Influence of Sea Power Upon History* 1600-1783. Boston : Little Brown, 1890.

Menon, Kumara Padmanabha Sivasundara, *The Indo-Soviet Treaty : Setting and Meaning.* Delhi : Vikas Publications, 1971.

Millar, T.B., *Soviet Policies in the Indian Ocean Area.* Canberra Papers on Strategy and Defence, no. 7. Canberra : Australian National University Press, 1970.

— — —, ed., *Britain's Withdrawal from Asia. Its Implications for Australia.* Canberra : Strategic and Defense Studies Centre, Australian National University, 1967.

Mishra, D.P., *Living an Era,* Vols. I and II, Vikas Publishing House Pvt. Ltd., New Delhi, 1975, 1978.

Misra, K.P. (ed.), *Janata Government's Foreign Policy.* Vikas Publishing House, New Delhi : 1979.

Naik, J.A., *Soviet Policy Towards India from Stalin to Brezhnev.* Delhi : Vikas Publications, 1970.

Namboodri, P.K.S. et al., *Intervention in the Indian Ocean*. New Delhi : ABC Publishing House, 1982.

Neelkant, K., *Partner in Peace. A Study of Indo-Soviet Relations.* Delhi : Vikas Publications, 1972.

Nehru, Jawaharlal, *India's Foreign Policy,* Publications Division, Govt, of India, 1961.

Nitze, Paul H. et al., *Securing the Seas : The Soviet Naval Challenge and Western Alliance Options*. Boulder, Colorado : Westview Press, 1979.

Nutting, Anthony, *No End of a Lesson : The Story of Suez.* London : Constable, 1967.

Panikkar, K.M., *Asia and Western Dominance*. London : Allen & Unwin, 1959.

———, *India and the Indian Ocean*. London : Allen & Unwin, 1945.

— — —, *Malabar and the Portuguese*. Bombay : D.B. Taraporevala Sons, 1929.

Poulose, T.T. ed., *Indian Ocean Power Rivalry*. New Delhi : Young Asia Publications, 1974.

Riedl, Harold A., *The Indian Ocean Power Vacuum*. Report no. 4701, April, 9172. Air War College, Air University. Alabama : Maxwell Air Force Base, 1972.

Rohwer, Jurgen, *Superpower Confrontation on the Seas : Naval Development and Strategy Since 1945.* Beverly Hills, CA. : Sage Publications, 1975.

Sharma, Shri Ram, *Indian Foreign Policy Annual Survey, 1981-1988.*

Sidhu, K.S., *Indian Ocean : A Zone of Peace, A Study of Indian Viewpoint*. New Delhi : 1983.

Singh, K.R., *Politics of the Indian Ocean*, New Delhi : 1974.

— — —, *The Indian Ocean : Big Power Presence and Local Response*. New Delhi : 1977.

Stein, Arthur Benjamin, *India and the Soviet Union : The Nehru Era*. Chicago : University of Chicago Press, 1969.

Tahtinen, Dale R., *Arms in the Indian Ocean : Interests and Challenges.* Washington, D.C. : American Enterprise Institute for Public Policy Research, 1977.

Thompson, Edward and G.T. Garratt, *Rise and Fulfilment of British Rule in India.* New York : AMS Press, 1971.

Thomson, George C., *Problems of Strategy in the Pacific and Indian Oceans.* New York : National Strategy Information Center, 1970.

Toussaint, A., *History of the Indian Ocean.* Translated by June Guicharnaud. Chicago : University of Chicago Press, 1966.

Towle, Philip, *Naval Power in the Indian Ocean : Threats, Bluffs, and Fantasies.* Canberra : Strategic and Defense Studies Centre, Australian National University, 1979.

Vaidya, K.B., *The Naval Defence of India.* Bombay : Thacker & Co., 1949.

Vali, Ferenc A., *Politics of the Indian Ocean Region : The Balance of Power.* New York : Free Press, 1976.

Van der Kroef, Justus M., *Australian Security Policies and Problems.* New York : National Strategy Information Center, 1970

Vichakar, Jagdish, *Afro-Asian Security and the Indian Ocean.* New Delhi : Sterling Publishers, 1974.

Villiers, Alan, *The Indian Ocean.* London : Museum Press, 1952.

Vincent, William, *The Commerce and Navigation of the Ancients in the Indian Ocean.* London : T. Cadell and W. Davies, 1807.

Wall, Patrick ed., *The Indian Ocean and the Threat to the West: Four Studies in Global Strategy.* London : Stacey International, 1975.

Wilcox, Wayne Ayres., *Nuclear Weapon Options and the Strategic Environment in South Asia :* Arms Control Implications for India. Santa Monica, C.A. : Southern California Arms Control and Foreign Policy Seminar, 1972.

Zafar, Imam, *Ideology and Reality in Soviet Policy in Asia: Indo-Soviet Relations.* Delhi : Kalyani Publishers, 1975.

Articles

Alford, Jonathan, 'Strategic Developments in the Indian Ocean Area'. *Asian Affairs* (London),68 (June,1979) : 141-9.

Anand, J.P., 'Big Powers and the Indian Ocean'. *The Institute of Defence Studies and Analysis Journal,* 8 (April-June, 1976) : 569-602.

Atkinson, James D., 'Who Will Dominate the Strategic Indian Ocean Area in the 1970s ? ' *Sea Power,* 11 (September, 1968) : 22-6.

Bukaramber, Bukar, 'Zone of Peace or Strategic Primacy : Politics of Security in the Indian Ocean'. *Bulletin of Peace Proposals,* 16 no. 1 (1985) : 51-60.

Burt, Richard, 'Strategic Politics and the Indian Ocean'. *Pacific Affairs,* 47 (Winter 1975-6) : 509-14.

Chari, P.R., 'The Indian Ocean : Strategic Issues'. *International Studies,* 18 (April-June, 1979) : 163-76.

— — —, 'The Indian Ocean : An Indian Viewpoint'. *Iranian Review of International Relations,* 8 (Fall 1976) : 163-84.

Cottrell, Alvin J., 'Indian Ocean of Tomorrow'. *Sea Power,* 25 (March,1971) : 10-16.

Darby, Phillip, 'Beyond East of Suez'. *International Affairs,* 46 (October, 1970) : 655-9.

Das, D.P., 'India and the Indian Ocean : A Study of Past and Future Strategy'. *China Report,* 10 (January-April,1974): 55-70.

Fuller, Jack, 'Dateline Diego Garcia : Paved-over Paradise'. *Foreign Policy,* 28 (Fall 1977) : 175-86.

Furlong, R.D.M., 'Strategic Power in the Indian Ocean'. *International Defense Review* (April, 1972) : 133-40.

Gerosa, Guide, 'Will the Indian Ocean Become a Soviet Pond ? *Atlas,* 19 (November, 1970) : 20-1.

Gill, Graeme F., 'The Soviet Union, Detente and the Indian Ocean'. *Australian Outlook,* 31 (August, 1977) : 253-60.

Griffith, William E., 'The Great Powers, the Indian Ocean, and the Persian Gulf'. *Jerusalem Journal of International Relations,* 1 (Winter 1975) : 5-19.

Hutchison, Alan, 'Indian Ocean : The Island Viewpoint'. *Africa Report*, 20 (January-February, 1975) : 52-4.

Jukes, Geoffrey. 'The Soviet Union and the Indian Ocean'. *Survival,* 13 (November,1971) : 370-5.

Khan, Rashid Ahmad, 'India's Indian Ocean Policy : Origins and Development'. *Strategic Studies,* 6 (Summer 1983) : 50-61.

Klare, Michael T., 'Superpower Rivalry at Sea'. *Foreign Policy* (Winter 1975) : 86-96, 160-7.

Kumar, Chandra, 'The Indian Ocean : Arc of Crisis or Zone of Peace ?, *International Affairs,* 60 (Spring, 1984) : 233-46.

Larus, Joel, 'The End of Naval Detente in the Indian Ocean'. *The World Today,* 36 (April, 1980) : 126-32.

Lebedev, Igor A., 'Soviet Policy Considerations Regarding the Indian Ocean'. *Australian Outlook,* 31 (April, 1977) : 133-42.

Madeley, John, 'Diego Garcia : An Indian Ocean Storm-Centre'. *The Round Table,* 283 (July, 1981) : 253-7.

Misra, K.P., 'Developments in the Indian Ocean Area : the Littoral Response'. *International Studies,* 16 (January-March, 1977) : 17-34.

Mugomba, Agrippah T., 'Indian Ocean as a Zone of Peace : An African Perspective'. *Alternatives*, 4 (July, 1979) : 115-33.

Nayar, Baldev Raj, 'Treat India Seriously'. *Foreign Policy*, 18 (Spring 1975) : 133-54.

Paone, R.M., 'The Big Three and the Indian Ocean'. *Sea Power*, 18 (August, 1975) : 28-34.

Parker, J.A., 'Indian Ocean : A New Soviet Lake ?' *New Guard,* 15 (March, 1975) : 7-10.

Pavlovsky, V. and Y. Tomilin, 'Indian Ocean : Confrontation or Security ?' *New Times* (Moscow), 10 (March,1974) : 4-5.

Prina, L. Edger, 'At Last, a Base in the Indian Ocean'. *Sea*

Power, 14 (January, 1971) : 26-8.

Rais, Rasul B., 'An Appraisal of US Strategy in the Indian Ocean'. *Asian Survey* (September, 1983) : 1043-51.

Ramchandani, R.R., 'Superpower Rivalry in Africa and the Indian Ocean'. *Foreign Affairs Reports*, 31 (February, 1982) : 39-47.

Richard, Jr., A. Best, 'Indian Ocean Arms Control'. *US Naval Institute Proceedings*, 106/2/024 (February, 1980) : 42-8.

Seth, S.P., 'The Indian Ocean and Indo-American Relations'. *Asian Survey*, 15 (August, 1975) : 645-55.

Shanti, Sadiq Ali, 'India and the Indian Ocean'. *Foreign Affairs Reports*, 31 (February, 1982) : 22-8.

Sharma, R.C., 'International and Regional Focus on the Indian Ocean'. *Pacific Community*, 7 (April, 1976) : 433-57.

Sim, J.P., 'Soviet Naval Presence in the Indian Ocean', *Australian Outlook*, 31 (April, 1977) : 185-92.

Speed, F.W., 'Indian Ocean Rivalry'. *Army Quarterly and Defense Journal*, 105 (October, 1975) : 457-63.

Stone, Norman L., 'An Indian Ocean Fleet - The Case and the Cost', *US Naval Institute Proceedings*, 107 (July, 1981): 54-7.

Vigor, P.H., 'Admiral S.G. Gorshkov's Views on Seapower'. *Journal of the Royal United Services Institute for Defence Studies*, 119 (March, 1974) : 53-60.

Vivekanandan, B., 'The Indian Ocean as a Zone of Peace : Problems and Prospects'. *Asian Survey*, 21 (June, 1981): 1237-49.

Wheeler, Geoffrey, 'The Indian Ocean Area : Soviet Aims and Interests', *Asian Affairs*, 59 (October, 1972) : 270-4.

Wingerter, Rax, 'The United States, the Soviet Union, and the Indian Ocean : The Competition for the Third World'. *Bulletin of Concerned Asian Scholars*, 9 (July-September, 1977) : 52-64.

Yefremov, V., 'The Indian Ocean : Confrontation Arena or Peace Zone ?' *Soviet Military Review*, 4 (April, 1981) : 50-1.

Zakheim, Dov S., 'Towards a Western Approach to the Indian Ocean'. *Survival*, 22 (January-February, 1980) : 7-14.

Index